Tarleton's Southside Raid

and Peter Francisco's famous fight

Colonel Greg Eanes
U.S. Air Force, Retired

Copyright © 2014 Greg Eanes
The Eanes Group, LLC
105 Guy Ave., Crewe, Va 23930
All rights reserved.

A Virginia Certified
Service Disabled Veteran Owned Small Business
(SWAM #709249)

ISBN: 1495949478
ISBN-13: 978-1495949470

TARLETON'S SOUTHSIDE RAID

The definitive history of British Colonel Banastre Tarleton's Southside Virginia Raid (July 9-July 24, 1781) to destroy Virginia military and Continental supply depots at Amelia Court House, Prince Edward Court House, Charlotte Court House and Bedford during the Yorktown Campaign of the American Revolution.

Sources include official records, period correspondence and recorded oral tradition.

This second edition has been updated with additional information and has been reformatted

CONTENTS

	Acknowledgments	i
1	Prelude to Yorktown	9
2	The Raid	25
3	The Militia Mobilizes	47
4	The Return Trip	61
5	The Fallout	79
6	Annex A-Logistics Targets	89
7	Annex B-Calendar July 1781	93
8	Annex C-Auto Tour	95
9	Annex D-Peter Francisco	99
10	Bibliography & Notes	107

Greg Eanes

ACKNOWLEDGEMENTS

No work is ever started without some seed of inspiration that germinates until it takes root. With that in mind, an acknowledgement should be made to the Amelia-Nottoway (Va) James Allen Chapter of the Daughters of the American Revolution (DAR) whose work in preserving locally the story of Peter Francisco's heroic fight at Ward's Tavern (near Crewe, Va) has been a primary mission.

During the Bicentennial celebrations, the James Allen Chapter, with others, was instrumental in getting March 15th proclaimed by the Governor as Peter Francisco Day in Virginia. They also facilitated, with help from Jim R. Eanes, editor of <u>The Crewe-Burkeville Journal</u>, the Crewe-Burkeville Chamber of Commerce, the Town of Crewe, and the Society of Descendants of Peter Francisco, a Peter Francisco Festival that involved the entire community. These events served to open the eyes of a great many young people (myself among them) to their local American Revolutionary heritage.

What I learned much later was that the Francisco event was merely one episode in a larger military operation: Tarleton's Southside Raid. Hopefully this work will help put the Francisco event and other regional vignettes in some historical context.

Greg Eanes
Crewe, Va

Greg Eanes

1 PRELUDE TO YORKTOWN

After the March 15, 1781 Revolutionary War battle of Guilford Court House (NC), British commander Lord Charles Cornwallis was forced to withdraw to the coast for supplies and reinforcements. Cornwallis realized American General Nathanael Greene's partisan war was taking a toll in British lives. He determined the best way to destroy Greene's army and subdue the south was to destroy the breadbasket state – Virginia—which provided short term militia reinforcements and met patriot supply needs with salt, flour, ammunition and tobacco for foreign credit.

Figure 1 Lord Charles Cornwallis

Cornwallis marched to Petersburg with 1,500 troops where in May he joined other British forces that had been raiding along the James River under the various commands of Brigadier General Benedict Arnold and Major General William Phillips.

Cornwallis arrived in Petersburg just after the death of Phillips and was soon reinforced with 1,200 troops from the North, swelling the total British ranks in Virginia to 7,200 men. This newly enlarged force began operations in late May north of the James River reaching Charlottesville in June. It was opposed by a small group of American regulars and Virginia militia under the Marquis de Lafayette. Another force of regulars under General Anthony Wayne arrived in June to assist Lafayette.

From May to July Cornwallis maneuvered with the main American force under Lafayette in an effort to trap and defeat it. Cornwallis was soon ordered by Sir Henry Clinton (overall British commander in North America) to concentrate British forces on the coast, send reinforcements to New York and establish a base of operations around Gloucester and Yorktown. Clinton was afraid Washington was going to attempt to capture New York and wanted to fend off that threat while Cornwallis established a British base in Virginia.

Figure 2 Major General Lafayette

Clinton felt Cornwallis could, from a fortified coastal position, conduct forays into Virginia's interior designed to wreak havoc upon the supply and manufacturing depots of the Continental armies as well as the tobacco Virginia used for international trade. The mission was to keep Virginia troops occupied in Virginia and deny reinforcements to Washington or Greene, deny the main American armies needed supplies and, if possible, draw Greene's Army into Virginia and away from British outposts in the Carolinas.

Cornwallis had been conducting operations with these objectives in mind. As early as June 11, while near Charlottesville, Cornwallis issued orders to Tarleton to destroy all stores of tobacco and corn between the Dan and James Rivers as well as intercept and disperse the regiment of 18-months men Baron Friedrich von Steuben was attempting to train as reinforcements for Green's Southern Army. The threat of Lafayette's and Anthony Wayne's combined forces caused this order to be rescinded and Tarleton retreated down country with the main body. On July 6, prior to crossing the James River at Jamestown, Cornwallis lured Lafayette into a trap resulting in the battle of Green Spring. Quick action by Anthony Wayne created a way for the Americans to escape decimation.[1]

Figure 3 Nathanael Greene

Upon crossing the James River, Cornwallis saw an opportunity to continue the destruction of American supplies. British forces had been successful in destroying the Virginia Navy and small water craft along the James River giving the British control of that line of communication. The majority of the militia were mobilized on the north side of the James and Cornwallis guessed it would be "difficult" for the Americans to counteract any British operations on the south side of the James. With this in mind, he planned three raids for the south side. These included a raid on South Quay in the Dismal Swamp, a raid on Edenton, NC and Tarleton's raid through Southside Virginia. A fourth raid tentatively scheduled up the Potomac to further stretch the militia's ability to respond was cancelled.[2] There is no evidence to suggest the Edenton Raid occurred either.

Cornwallis instructed Tarleton in a letter from the village of Cobham (near the present day Jamestown Ferry) on July 8 to:

"begin your march tomorrow with the corps of cavalry and mounted infantry under your command to Prince Edward Court House, and from thence to New London in Bedford County, making the strictest inquiry in every part of the country through which you pass, for ammunition, clothing, or stores of any kind, intended for the public; and as there is no pressing service for your corps in this provence, I must desire you will be in no haste to return; but do everything in your power to destroy the supplies destined for the rebel army.

"All public stores of corn and provisions are to be burnt and if there should be a quantity of provisions of corn collected at a private house, I would have you destroy it, even although there should be no proof of its

being intended for the public service, leaving enough for the support of the family, as there is the greatest reason to apprehend that such provisions will be ultimately appropriated by the enemy to the use of General Greene's army, which, from the present state of the Carolinas, must depend on this province [Virginia] for its supplies."

Cornwallis anticipated Green might even swing into Virginia to counter the British threat there. "As it is very probable," he wrote, "that some of the light troops of General Greene's army may be on their return to this country, you will do all you can to procure intelligence of their route; I need not tell you of what importance it will be to intercept them, or any prisoners of ours from South Carolina. I would have all persons of consequence, either civil or military, brought to me before they are paroled."

Cornwallis issued three light wagons to carry captured goods as well as "a puncheon of rum." Tarleton was also ordered to conduct a form of psychological operations by telling local citizens that his force was the advance guard of the main British army. This misinformation might serve to draw off Greene, now heading into South Carolina to attack isolated British outposts there. Tarleton was also to "order, under pain of military execution, the people of the country to provide wagons, etc, to expedite the movements of my army.

"Most sincerely wishing you success," Cornwallis ended his order, "and placing the greatest confidence in your zeal and abilities." Tarleton's zeal and abilities were well known to both his commander and the American patriots. They were traits that struck fear among men unaccustomed to the barbarities of war.[3]

Banastre Tarleton

Tarleton was born 21 August 1754 in Liverpool. In 1775, he was commissioned a Cornet of Dragoons and reached the war in America in 1776. He distinguished himself in various operations attaining the rank of Lieutenant Colonel of the British Legion by late 1778. He went to the

Figure 4 Tarleton by John Andre'

southern theater in 1780 and earned a reputation as a violent cavalry leader. Unlike the war in the north, the southern theater took on the tone of a vicious civil war where local communities turned on each other. During the ferocious close quarter fighting at the battle of the Waxhaws, Tarleton reportedly sabered a Continental Ensign as the man was raising a white flag of surrender. About this time Tarleton's own horse was shot from under him and many of his men thought he'd been killed. According to Tarleton, this event "stimulated the soldiers to a vindictive asperity not easily restrained."[4]

The Americans saw it differently. According to one Patriot witness:

> *"the demand for quarters…was at once found to be in vain; not a man was spared, and it was the concurrent testimony of all the survivors that for fifteen minutes after every man was prostrate they [British soldiers] went over the ground plunging their bayonets into every one that exhibited any signs of life, and in some instances where several had fallen over the other, these monsters were seen to throw off on the point of a bayonet the uppermost to come at those beneath."[5]*

Another American reportedly received 23 wounds to include having his hand chopped off and several bayonet thrusts to his body. He refused to surrender and survived the battle. From this time on 'Tarleton's Quarter" came to be known to Americans as the slaughter of captured men. The 26-year old Tarleton's reputation, whether or not earned or deserved, was spread.

While the battle of the Waxhaws, also known as Buford's defeat, was brutal and bloody, there is some question as to whether the slaughter was instigated by Tarleton or just evolved from the circumstances of the battle. Tarleton was known for his zeal and commitment but also his professionalism. This professionalism and perhaps humanitarianism was testified to by at least one Virginia pensioner, Benjamin Shenault who was among Buford's command. Shenault was taken prisoner and said he:

> *"was permitted by Colonel Tarlton (sic), who commanded the British troops that defeated [Buford], to remain with the wounded Americans for the purpose of attending on them until (sic) their recovery: This duty he performed with five other soldiers, all of whom as well as himself were left on parole by the British officer above named...."[6]*

According to one early British military observer:

> *"Tarleton was a remarkable soldier with an instinctive talent for war. He achieved his successes, usually at very small cost, by the secrecy of his operations, the high standard of training of his officers and men, and by his own skill and daring in action. He fought with the object[of] inflicting every possible loss and injury on his enemy, and he has been accused of undue harshness, and even of cruelty. American writers have gone so far as to describe him as 'a devil incarnate,' but the same writers call Lord Cornwallis, an exceptionally humane soldier, 'a relentless savage.' Such unmeasured language loses all effect, and leaves no stain on the persons attacked."[7]*

The British Legion

Tarleton's 'British Legion' were actually American Provincials who had remained loyal to the King. The Caledonian Volunteers comprised part of the Legion. The Volunteers were 151 partly mounted and part infantry raised in Philadelphia in late 1777 and attached to the British Army in New York the following year under the command of Captain William Sutherland. In July 1778 the Caledonians merged with

three other companies of Tories to comprise the
British Legion totaling 773 men. They were sent to
Savannah in December 1779 and served with
Cornwallis throughout the Southern Campaigns.
Attrition whittled the force down until the debacle at
Cowpens where Daniel Morgan decimated Tarleton's
force including his vaunted Legion. Tarleton managed
to escape and reorganize a force of about 350 men
after Cowpens. It was said the men in the unit
provided the best horses for the cavalry "by stealing
race horses from the plantations of Virginia and the
Carolinas."[8]

Just prior to the Southside raid, the members of the
British Legion Cavalry were identified to be placed on
the Regular Establishment which entitled them to the
same pay and benefits of regular British soldiers. They
wore a distinctive green jacket as part of their uniform
and made a name for themselves through their raids
through the Carolinas. Four months prior to the
Southside raid, at the battle of Guilford Court House,
Tarleton's British Legion numbered 180 cavalry and
172 infantry for a total of 354 troops. By the time of
the June 1781 Charlottesville raid to capture Thomas
Jefferson, Tarleton was down to 180 dragoons and 70
mounted infantry for about 250 troops.

For the Southside raid Tarleton records that he took
only the Legion cavalry and 80 mounted infantry.
Using Guilford Court House cavalry figures, it is
possible Tarleton started on this raid with 260 troops
though at least one eyewitness, Peter Francisco,
estimated as many as 400 British soldiers were
involved in the raid. The mounted infantry are

believed to have come from the 23rd Regiment of Foot also known as the Royal Welsh Fusiliers.[9]

The psychological effect of Legion atrocities, real and imagined, on Americans was one that caused American unity out of fear of the British. Many potential neutrals joined the patriot cause and many undisciplined militia would stand and fight rather than attempt to run or surrender knowing capture meant death at the hands of Tarleton's dragoons. Reported Legion cruelties solidified patriot resistance. With this background behind him, Tarleton led his force into Virginia's southern interior.

The Terrain
The area known as Southside is generally that part of Virginia on 'the south side' of the James River. This river stretches from the coastal lowlands (known as Tidewater) through the rolling hills of the Piedmont to a confluence with the Rivanna River in the Blue Ridge Mountains. There are a variety of streams and rivers that drain into the James River Basin. A major tributary is the Appomattox River which joins the James at Petersburg and is navigable by canoe and bateaux through Chesterfield and Amelia Counties to Prince Edward County. The tributaries to both rivers vary in size.

Navigation of the James River from the mountains to the falls above Richmond was by bateaux. In Colonial days trade goods were transferred to larger ships in Richmond for transport downriver and various ports. The lower James was passable only by watercraft, usually a ferry of some kind. By July 1781 British control of this vital sea lane prevented American forces from making rapid or large scale crossings to concentrate against British military threats north or south of the James. As a result, small bodies of militia covered both sides of the mouth of the lower James (primarily for observation) while the main forces under Lafayette and Anthony Wayne remained just east of Richmond. This put the main Continental Army in a position to deploy to suitable crossings by short marches north or south as dictated by Cornwallis' maneuvers or to meet Cornwallis head-on should he attempt to travel up the James again. The American inability to use ships (due to British naval superiority) in the lower James precluded timely responses to real and perceived British military threats. American military mobility was further hampered by the lack of an organized and dedicated corps of dragoons. The dragoon situation would correct itself but not before Tarleton began his raid in the Southside.

Figure 5 Tarleton

Figure 6 TARLETON'S AUTOGRAPH - from an 8 December 1798 letter. (Preston Davie Collection, 1560-1903, Folder 273, Southern Historical Collection, The Wilson Library, University of North Carolina at Chapel Hill.)

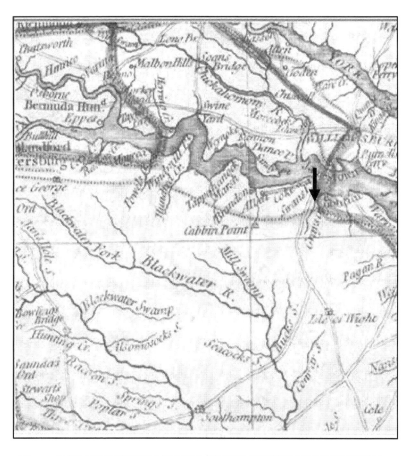

Figure 7 TARLETON'S MARCH FROM COBHAM TO PRINCE GEORGE COURT HOUSE. – This image (the southernmost dark dotted line) shows Tarleton's route from Cobham (at arrow) to the west, along the south side of the James River roughly correlating to modern Virginia Rt. 10. This was also his return route to Portsmouth. There's little to suggest he did much damage until he arrived in Amelia County (not depicted). (Reference: LC Maps of North America, 1750-1789, 1409)

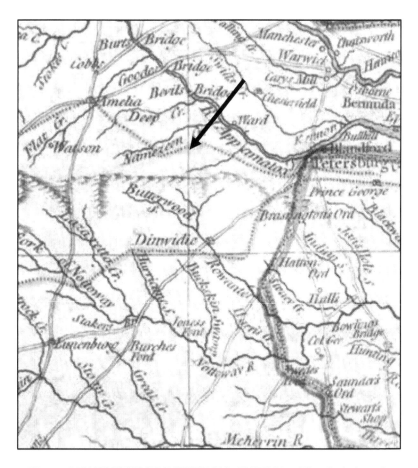

Figure 8 TARLETON'S ROUTE TO AMELIA – The dark dotted line from Petersburg to Amelia shows Tarleton's infiltration. The community annotation of 'Watson' is near present-day Crewe. Francisco's fight would have occurred just northeast of this point towards the old Amelia Court House. The arrow points to the line of travel.

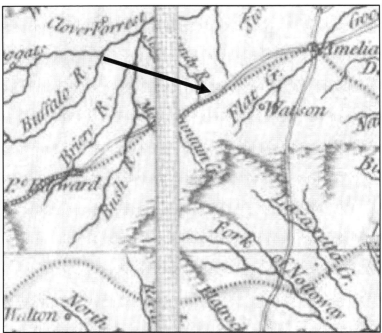

Figure 9 TARLETON'S ROUTE TO PRINCE EDWARD – The dark dotted line from Amelia shows Tarleton's route to Prince Edward Court House, the site of modern day Worsham. Near the centerline, and partially obscured is the Sandy River crossing the main road. This intersection is about two miles from Millers (Burke's Tavern) where Tarleton encamped. This route corresponds with the modern day Sandy River Road in Prince Edward. The arrow points to the line of travel and approximate location of Miller's (Burke's) Tavern.

Greg Eanes

2 THE RAID

Tarleton started westward on the morning of July 9, 1781. Because the July heat was exhausting on both horses and men, he conducted the march "by long movements in the morning and evening; By which means the heat and darkness were as much as possible avoided, and time afforded for refreshment and repose."[10]

He reached Petersburg and created some alarm in the Virginia War Office in Richmond. According to the War Office Journal for July 11, 1781, a letter was dispatched to Baron Steuben, then recruiting troops for the Continental Line in Virginia, "informing him of the enemy's light troops being at Petersburg, the Maquis at Holt's Forge and the Executive at this place [Richmond]." The War Office added they had no guards, no videttes or express riders to provide warning should Tarleton advance on that place.[11]

Tarleton continued west eventually arriving at Amelia, in the West Creek area, where they burned a mill owned by Daniel Jones at 'Mt. Airy'. The mill and granary was constructed by Jones in 1780 and in April 1781, Continental authorities seized it to use in support of government activities to provide food the army. According to Jones, "on the 13th day of July…whilst the said Mill and Houses were occupied by them in the public service, a party of the enemy commanded by Lieut. Col. Tarleton came up and burned the said mill and houses to the ground."[12]

The British raiders reportedly traveled on the Namozine Road and traveled through Mannboro and old Amelia Court House, located now in Nottoway County on the Amelia-Nottoway boundary. While here they reportedly burned all or part of the records. They also burned a granary on the Richmond road near Mannboro.[13]

At least one area man identified as Charles Knight was "referred to as a Tory and haborer of Tarleton."[14] Tarleton reportedly made a temporary headquarters at the Knight's residence which was in Burkeville. Reports of movements and actions in the vicinity suggests Tarleton established headquarters there and sent out detachments to destroy public property and capture civil or military persons of local prominence. One group of British raiders captured local resident James Cooke, then a young boy, near his home in Jennings's Ordinary. He was made to ride on a horse behind one of the dragoons who carried him to Tarleton's headquarters. On the way over the British soldier took Cooke's shoe and knee buckles against the boy's objections. When they got to headquarters Cooke complained to Tarleton who ordered the items returned and the boy was sent on his way. The British soldier ambushed Cooke after he started for home and stole the items again.[15]

In the vicinity of Jennings Ordinary, on West Creek, stood the tavern of Benjamin Ward. His wife feared the rumored appearance of the British Army and decided to take her children a son, Benjamin, and a daughter) to family in Charlotte County. A black driver known as Joe was with them.

According to one version of the story, the group:

"went in a chariot with four horses when they were surprised at the forks of the road between Burkeville and Crewe by a party of dragoons. The boy was carefully concealed in some of the crannies or lurking places old-fashioned vehicles afforded before they were halted.

"The dragoons seized the baggage, taking out the silks and satins and cutting them into ribbons with their bayonets, hold[ing] them upon the points to show their forlorn condition.

"The horses were seized and the helpless family was about to be left in the road when old Joe, the driver, fell upon his knees and begged that he be allowed two of the horses to continue the journey.

"His pleading was so far successful that he was allowed to take two of his own horses back to the chariot or to have two of the cavalry horses instead…he was a weaver and went by the name of Joe Weaver.

"At the time of this outrage, an ancestor of the Royal family of Nottoway was also in the highway in danger of marauders. But more lucky than Mrs. Ward, he saw the approach and concealed himself in the thick boughs of a tree just where the roads make a turn that he might gauge their movements. He saw the halt and the pillage of the carriage was not discovered."

A family version of the story goes as follows:

> *"When Tarleton was raiding South Side Virginia in 1781, Catherine Ward decided to take her most valuable silver, jewels, and silks to Ward's Fork [Charlotte County] where she hoped they would be safe from the hands of the marauding British. With only the chair driver and her small son, Benjamin, she set forth on her journey, a long one for that mode of transportation and the roads of that day. When she came to where Burkeville now stands, to her utter dismay, Tarleton's men were across the road ahead of her! Under the seat went little Benjamin. Nobody troubled him but [Catherine's] fate was sadder. The soldiers took her silver and jewels, riddled her silks and marched off with them on the points of their swords."*[16]

Another story goes that a Mr. Verser who lived in the same part of the county saw the dragoons, got down from his horse, waded into one of the mill ponds of which the county was full, and secreted himself until they passed by." An unidentified brother of Captain Joseph Fowlkes also reportedly saw the incident from a nearby tree-op. It is reported the British dragoons "went off with silks on the points of their swords."[17]

A group of them in the vicinity of present-day Crewe "flushed Colonel William Craddock…The British pursued him from his home in hot haste until he was forced to take shelter, with his horse, in a barn on the road to Jetersville. Here the troops passed him, but he was fearful lest his horse should neigh to those passing and so reveal his presence. He escaped."[18]

On July 11 or 12, the raiders destroyed a dwelling that

served as a house and a store for Thomas Griffin Peachy of Rocky Run in Amelia as well as 600 to 700 bushels of wheat reported as public property.

Francisco's Fight

Figure 10 FRANCISCO'S ENCOUNTER WITH NINE BRITISH DRAGOONS - This image in Howe's History has a cutline that says, "This representation of Peter Francisco's gallant action with nine of Tarleton's cavalry, in sight of a troop of 400 men, which took place in Amelia County, Virginia, 1781, is respectfully inscribed to him by James Webster and artist James Warrell. Published Dec. 1st, 1814 by James Webster of Pennsylvania." This image or versions of it were massed produced and hung over many fireplace mantles in the period.

While in this area "a plundering party of British detached from the main body of Tarleton's command" and visited Ward's Tavern along West Creek with the intention of "plunder." one of the guests happened to be Peter Francisco who was reportedly on a scouting mission though he was still recovering from serious wounds received at the battle of Guilford Court House four months earlier.[19]

When Francisco stepped outside the tavern, he was surprised by nine of Tarleton's dragoons who were accompanied by three negroes. These men were probably the advance of the main body. Francisco was made their prisoner. Being outnumbered and unarmed, Francisco could only acquiesce to the demands of his captors. According to the account written by Henry Howe in 1845, the soldiers believed Francisco to be a peaceful captive so they left one man outside while the rest went in the tavern for refreshment. The dragoon, identified as the paymaster, reportedly told Francisco, "Give up instantly all that you possess of value...or prepare to die."

"I have nothing to give up," Francisco declared, "so use your pleasure." (In one account he claims he gave up a watch.)

The soldier rejoined, "Deliver instantly those massive silver buckles which you wear on your shoes."

"They were a present from a valued friend," replied Francisco, "and it would grieve me to part with them. Give them into your hands I never will. You have the power to take them, if you think fit."

"The soldier put his sabre under his arm, and bent

down to take them'," Howe recorded, "Francisco, finding so favorable an opportunity to recover his liberty, stepped one pace in his rear, drew the sword with force from under his arm, and instantly gave him a blow across the scull (sic).

"My enemy," observed Francisco, "was brave and though severely wounded, drew a pistol, and, in the same moment that he pulled the trigger, I cut his hand nearly off. The bullet grazed my side. Ben Ward (the man of the house) very ungenerously brought out a musket, and gave it to one of the British soldiers, and told him to make use of that. He mounted the only horse they could get, and present[ed] it [the musket] at my breast. It missed fire. I rushed on the muzzle of the gun. A short struggle ensued. I disarmed and wounded him. Tarleton's troop of four hundred men were in sight.

"All was hurry and confusion, which I increased by repeatedly hallooing, as loud as I could, "Come on, my brave boys, now's your time; we will soon dispatch these few, and then attack the main body!"

"The wounded men flew to the troops; others were panic struck, and fled. I seized Ward, and would have dispatched him, but the poor wretch begged for his life; he was not only an object of my contempt, but pity. The eight horses that were left behind, I gave him to conceal for me. Discovering that Tarleton had dispatched ten more in pursuit of me, I made off. I, like an old fox, doubled, and fell on their rear. I went the next day to Ward for my horses; he demanded two, for his trouble and generous intentions. Finding my situation dangerous, and surrounded by enemies where I ought to have friends, I went off with my six horses. I intended to have avenged myself at a future day, but Providence ordained I should not be his executioner for he broke his neck by a fall from one of the very horses."[20]

Francisco said the "ninth man escaped with a large cut upon his back. They all joined Tarleton, who was about a mile off, except the slain man. This is the last favor I ever did the British."[21]

During the brief fight, Francisco reportedly killed or mortally wounded three British soldiers. According to Francisco's son, Dr. B.M. Francisco, Tarleton offered a reward for Peter's capture.[22]

Francisco evaded to Prince Edward County where he spread the alarm regarding Tarleton's approach. Though Peter Francisco doesn't state (in the Howe account) where the British dragoons stopped to

Figure 11 DAR Memorial at West Creek remembering the legend.

Figure 12 PETER FRANCISCO'S FIGHT – Image published in December 1814. Engraving by David Edwin.

Figure 13 WARD's TAVERN AND HOMESTEAD –
Francisco's Fight occurred just a few feet in front of the main steps and was the original location of the DAR marker. The house burned 12 April 1902.

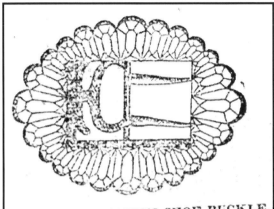

PETER FRANCISCO'S SHOE BUCKLE.

The above picture is an exact reproduction of an old shoe-buckle, silver, set with brilliants, which belonged to Peter Francisco, and which has been handed down in the family. It is owned by Mr. Henry Francisco, of this city, at the present time. The buckle is one of a pair worn by Francisco at the time of his great adventure with Tarleton's men in Amelia county.

Artist Drawing from 1901 *Richmond Dispatch*

refresh themselves, it may very well have been what became known as Burke's Tavern.[23] The tavern was situated on the main stage road between Jennings Ordinary and Prince Edward Court House (present day Worsham). Francisco sold the captured horses at Prince Edward Court House but kept one stallion which he named 'Tarleton' and rode it for many years.

One newspaperman remarked in 1907 of this event, "A thousand years ago, Francisco might have been canonized" for this feat.[24]

Though no exact dates are given, the incident at Ward's Tavern may have taken place on July 12, 1781. This date is assessed on the fact that the nearby Daniel Jones mill event took place on 12 July. Tarleton was moving in the cooler hours of the morning and late afternoon coupled with knowledge that Francisco was at Ward's to either stay overnight or having already stayed overnight. Further, the distance from Petersburg to Ward's Tavern is over forty miles which was about a hard day's ride. Tarleton reportedly averaged between 30 and 40 miles a day on this raid.

The Ward family disputed this version of the event. Benjamin Ward was a Captain of a local militia company and served in the Revolution. His nearby mill reportedly provided flour to the American Army and was likely destroyed by Tarleton's men.[25] Ben Ward, son of Captain Ward, in 1815 in the pages of the Richmond Enquirer challenged the Francisco account "saying that his father had not aided the enemy" providing affidavits of several men of the county to prove his case.[26]

Among the area places hit by Tarleton's dragoons was the Amelia home of Isaac Chapman. He was away on militia duty but reported years later that the property stolen by the raiders was a trunk containing, among other things, an honorable discharge from his first tour of duty in the Revolution.[27] Colonel William Craddock, a Revolutionary War officer, also "made a hairbreadth escape from the British on the public road near his house."[28]

Figure 14 Burke's (Miller's) Tavern today

Several prominent citizens were also taken captive. While some were paroled on the spot, others were kept in custody to include Colonel William Archer, commander of the Amelia County minute men and a man named Royall.[29]

At one point in this vicinity, Tarleton sought some rest. A local resident recalled Tarleton behaving "generously toward the inhabitants during the raid." He visited Captain Joe Fowlkes's mother, "a widow, who lived in Prince Edward a few miles above old Burkeville, and turned a chair down for a pillow and lay on the floor to rest. He set guards to watch and did not allow anything to be molested. He would always rebuke his men for depredations and in many instances showed a kind spirit."[30]

Tarleton proceeded through Jennings Ordinary reaching Miller's (later Burke's) Tavern where he reportedly encamped for the night.

General George Washington was well aware of Tarleton's earlier raids through Virginia and was concerned for the safety and security of the powder and ammunition magazines in Virginia's interior. On July 13 he wrote Lafayette, "Should the enemy confine themselves to the lower country, you will no doubt pay attention to the formation of Magazines above." He would not learn of Tarleton's Southside raid until July 20 in a letter from Lafayette.[31]

Supplies Moved

Some area militia took action to save supplies. Virginia veteran Jesse Stegall of Brunswick County was on a tour of duty to support foraging and subsistence for the army. The men he was with had gathered a "great many Beeves" and started to move them to Petersburg "for the army stationed there." He recalled:

> *"On the way [we] met a messenger at Dinwiddie [Court House] with orders to save the provisions. That the British Cavalry were coming on from Petersburg. We immediately hurried the Beeves to Amelia [Court House] – when we was there [we] learnt that the British were in pursuit – upon which Capt. Rivers [of Brunswick] ordered us to march to Capt. Booker's commissary, about 10 miles from Amelia Court House. The Beeves were delivered to Capt. Booker and our company permitted to discharge that day with order to rendezvous…in Brunswick early the next day."[32]*

Also in Amelia were about 70 horses destined for Continental service under the guard of Virginia militia. Powhatan County veteran Joseph Baugh recalled:

> *"we were again employed in keeping & guarding some public horses, and had upwards of seventy horses in our possession; and we remained there until we were informed that General Tarlton was approaching with his troop of horse & we then hastily fled, crossed at [Jude] s Ferry in Powhatan and joined the American army at the falls of James River a short distance above Richmond, where we delivered up the horses and were discharged."[33]*

Prince Edward Court House was a primary target on the raid. From February until March 1781, this part of Southside had been designated as a "special post" for collecting supplies and materials. From this location, the supplies could be distributed to Nathanael Greene's army in the Carolinas or to Lafayette's Continentals along the James River. The Southside counties of Prince Edward, Amelia, Dinwiddie, Chesterfield, Powhatan, Cumberland and Goochland were principal sources of flour for Lafayette's army that summer. His army required 50 barrels of flour a day. At least 40 wagons were needed to supply him.[34]

Also at Prince Edward was a "laboratory" for making gunpowder and ammunition. Sometime before July, the lab was moved because of the threat of British "partisans." Information suggests there was an active effort to move supplies out of the area before the British struck. A receipt for the period shows one John Calbreath received, from the Bedford County

Escheator, eight and one-half bushels of "public corn being for forage for two teams of horses employed in moving military stores from Prince Edward to Bedford Court House." Bedford Escheator records also show a decrease in receipted agricultural supplies for the five months after the raid compared with the four months preceding the raid suggesting the destruction of crops or harvested stockpiles by the British.[35]

Another record shows various people were paid for driving cattle away from the area on trips ranging from five to nine days in duration. Additionally the raid and the movement of supplies appears to have disrupted accurate record keeping. The Prince Edward Deputy Commissary's record book contains no entries from 1 July 1781 to 21 July 1781 which roughly equates to the dates of the raid in that area. Entries preceding and following those dates are available however.[36]

When the British dragoons got to Prince Edward on July 13th, they discovered the supply depot and ammunition factory had been moved. They did manage to break up a scheduled hanging at the court house however and camped in the immediate area. While there a party of British dragoons raided the glebe house of Rev. Archibald McRobert who had fled upon the soldiers' appearance. The dragoons reportedly "ripped open feather beds, broke mirrors, [and] set fire to the house on leaving." A sudden rain is supposed to have put the fire out thus sparing the house which, legend has it, cause the owner to rename the home Providence.[37]

McRobert later complained of Tarleton's actions in a letter to Governor Thomas Nelson. McRobert said, "Tarleton camped at his house, carried off five valuable negroes and all his horses. He left some worn out horses, one of which was claimed by the owner." He wanted to keep the rest of the worn out horses for farm work rather than turn them over to the government as strays.[38]

Tarleton is reported to have visited Slate Hill near Worsham, the home of Nathaniel Venable, the county commissary. The plantation was located on the 'Old Iroquois Trail' (present day State Route 15) which was the main road to the south.

The 48-year-old Venable was a former County Lieutenant[1] and member of the House of Burgesses. As the Revolution evolved, Venable became a member of the Prince Edward County Committee of Safety and was named 1st Lieutenant of militia in 1777. He was in the Virginia Senate in 1780. As a leading citizen he often advanced money for the purchase of salt, food and miscellaneous equipment and set an example of confidence in the new government by accepting Continental money for payment of goods.

Venable had already gone into hiding when Tarleton arrived. Because of the short notice, Mrs. Venable directed the hiding of plantation food supplies in tobacco hogsheads, "the hogsheads headed up, and all of them placed at the doors of the tobacco barns in

---

[1] **County Lieutenants held the rank of Colonel in the state militia and were responsible for all the county militia units.**

full view; hoping that this would disarm suspicion as to their contents. The manuevre worked; the hogsheads had every appearance of being innocent of food content." A twist on this story is that several empty hogsheads were stacked with the full barrels. The empty ones were left open and visible suggesting to observers the whole batch of hogsheads were empty.

Tradition further holds that when Tarleton's troopers went into the house, they demanded Mrs. Venable tell of her husband's whereabouts. The story goes, "upon her refusal to comply with the demand, one of the soldiers drew his pistol and threatened to shoot her unless she betrayed the secret. 'My husband has his country to defend; shoot,' she calmly replied. An officer intervened, and saved her life.[39]

In another local legend one John Davidson, a Guilford Court House veteran who had been wounded in the sword arm, went looking for the British, alone and armed only with a squirrel gun. At a point in his journey a British dragoon surprised Davidson and demanded he surrender. Davidson said he wasn't ready to surrender, raised his rifle with his left hand and shot the dragoon out of the saddle.

One source states, "Asked if he was satisfied with killing a single man, [Davidson] replied "By no means. I reloaded my piece and went in pursuit; but my firing had excited such alarm, and Tarleton fled with such expedition, that I never could have overtaken him, or I would have had another shot."[40]

This incident is similar to another recalled by John Hatchett, an eyewitness to Tarleton's visit to the area. Hatchett recalled:

> *"in the summer of '81 and a little after the wheat harvest, Col. Tarlton (sic) and his troop of Cavalry came in the neighborhood of Prince Edward Courthouse pillaging and burning as they came. Stayed all night at the Court House, went to several places pillaging as they went. Started for Charlotte [County] as [it] appeared, carrying all the men they got hold of prisners (sic) off with them and as they crossed Briery Bridge between Mr. Watson's and Mr. Allen's a brave young man that lived in the neighborhood stept in the road before them with his rifle well charged, ordering them to halt, and at the same time let fly among them, gave one his Mortall (sic) wound and made his escape, they then after coming as high as the forks of the road took the left hand leading to Moors Ordinary [Moore's Ordinary or present day Meherrin] taking all prisners (sic) they could get hold of along with them."*

Hatchett said the raiders "spent the Balance of that day at the Old Ordenary (sic) and then moved off, went through Lunenburgh, Brunswick and the lower counties, burning and plundering as they went to their headquarters. Soon after this the neighbors was alarmed again by a rumor that Cornwallis and his whole army was coming in the neighborhood." Hatchett also noted that a law had been passed requiring all males between the ages of 16 and 50 to shoulder arms.[41] Though Tarleton retreated through Moore's Ordinary, Hatchett's story does not account for Tarleton's continued travel through Charlotte to Bedford.

Tradition also has it that Tarleton visited the home of Captain James Wade. The home was called Mt. Airy and while there Tarleton reported left two cut glass decanters for the occupants.[42]

Another tradition says a dance was given for some of Tarleton's men at the Travis Plantation near Mt. Airy and the Sandy River Church. One of the dragoons dancing with a local girl reportedly said, "I have heard that Light-Horse Harry Lee is illiterate, that he can't read or write his name." Of rebel sympathies, the young woman, "observing a scar left on the officer's neck by Lee's sword during an encounter in the South" replied, "At least he can make his mark."[43]

At least one unnamed man at Prince Edward made a ride to give warning of the British Legion. One July 14, Colonel Hugh Rose of Amherst received a dispatch "telling him of the proposed [British] raids on Peytonsburg, New Glasgow (in Amherst) and New London (in Bedford, now Campbell County)." Col. Rose wrote to Major William Cabell, Jr., telling him that steps were being taken to protect the supplies. Another rider reportedly went south to warn General Greene.[44] Other men were also engaged in reconnaissance to keep track of Tarleton's movements.[45]

Figure 15 BURKE'S STORE -- Burke's Store adjacent Burke's/Miller's Tavern outside of Burkeville. This structure likely existed at the time of the Tarleton's visit. Before railroads, the stage lines would stop here to change out horses. The horses were kept in the bottom of this building while the top was occupied by a store that serviced the local community. This was on the main road between Prince Edward Court House and Amelia Court House.

3 THE MILITIA MOBILIZES

Meanwhile back in Richmond the Virginia Board of War issued a circular letter ordering the call up of more militia. One-seventh of the militia in Southside was ordered to mobilize and join Anthony Wayne "on his route southward, properly officered and equipped if possible. The whole rendezvous at Taylor's Ferry [on the Roanoke River between Charlotte and Halifax Counties] without loss of time." The militia of two counties were ordered directly to Greene and one-fourth of the militia in 37 other counties were ordered to report to Lafayette.[46]

One veteran serving with Wayne recalled, "after the engagement at Jamestown, it was said that British Col. Tarlton (sic) was advancing into Bedford County, Virginia for the purpose of taking the Public stores there." The veteran says he was marched under Wayne towards Bedford "for the purpose of repelling the attack of said Col. Tarleton" but halted "at the Bridge across the Appomattox River in the County of Amelia [when] news was received that Tarleton had retreated."[47]

July 15th dawned with expressions of concern among the Virginians for the safety of their stores. Major John Pryor, Field Commissary General of Military Stores in Charlottesville wrote Colonel William Davies saying:

> *"Mr. D. Ross [David Ross, Commercial Agent for Virginia] sent me an express with an account that they [the British] were at Amelia Court House on*

Thursday evening. I immediately sent off an Officer Express to New London, to have the whole of the military stores removed over the Ridge from that place. I sent an express to [Commissary General of Military Stores] Capt. [Ambrose] Bohannon also, and have called upon Major Claiborne, without success for wagons to be in readiness to remove the stores from this place. The Marquis has directed me to send 300 stand of arms to General [Robert] Lawson. If it was to save life, wagons could not be procured within a week – I am sick of the whole world."[48]

Lafayette was in Richmond on July 15 and also learned of the raiders. He immediately ordered General 'Mad Anthony' Wayne (then southeast of Richmond on the James River) to mobilize his forces to protect Richmond and, if the opportunity presented itself, to take on Tarleton. Lafayette wrote:

Figure 16 Anthony Wayne

"From the best intelligence I can get the enemy's cavalry have gone very high up in the country either with a view to destroy some stores or with the intention of gaining South Carolina. In either case it

becomes important that some troops be advanced further south, which may maneuver them lower down, or should the [Tarleton's] cavalry reinforce Lord Rawdon, form a junction with General Greene.

"General Morgan with the riflemen and what horse we can collect, will march tomorrow towards Goode's Bridge from Westham where he will cross the river. I request, you will tomorrow proceed to Chesterfield Courthouse, and the day following to Goode's Bridge. I have sent a commissary to lay in provisions at this place but it may be well for your commissary also to take precautions on the shores of Appomattox.

"General Morgan who proceeds you to Goode's Bridge will be able to inform you of the enemy's movements. Should a stroke at Col. Tarleton be found practicable you have my permission to make it in conjunction with General Morgan. But in case the enemy are going to the Southward you will be so far on your way to General Greene."[49]

On the same day the Governor's office issued circular letters to the various counties south and west of Richmond ordering the mobilization of more militia to proceed to General Wayne. The same letter ordered the other counties in Virginia to keep one-fourth of the militia in the field to support Lafayette then watching Cornwallis' main force.[50]

A position at Goode's Bridge on the Amelia-Chesterfield County line along the Appomattox River allowed Wayne and Morgan to establish a blocking position to protect Richmond and Lafayette from

Tarleton. This position also allowed Wayne to reinforce Lafayette should Cornwallis cross from Portsmouth and again march up the peninsula. It allowed him to move a short distance south to strike Tarleton should the British raiders come close enough to that location. And it placed him closer to Greene should he be required to move south to reinforce the Southern Army. Among the American forces concentrating at Goode's Bridge were Wayne's 500 Pennsylvanians, Gaskins Battalion of 300 Virginians and Morgan's Virginia Militia of about 500 plus an unknown number of militia cavalry with Morgan for a total of over 1,300 troops. Wayne's force took position on the Amelia side of the bridge while the Virginians remained on the north or Chesterfield side of the bridge. They would remain in place for about ten days awaiting the outcome of events. It was Lafayette's intention to send Wayne's force south to Greene if Cornwallis made for New York or detached Tarleton to the South.[51]

Figure 17 Daniel Morgan

On this day the raiders moved to the supply depot in Charlotte County. The depot should have been of considerable size as Charlotte supported a militia force of 565 rank and file, many of whom were already attached to Greene or Lafayette, leaving few to repulse the British raiding party. Tarleton's men found the military store there had also been moved.

Nevertheless, they reportedly burned tobacco and looted private property.

Colonel Josiah Parker, commanding an American partisan corps in the Tidewater area, wrote a letter to Lafayette to pass on information received from another source of Tarleton's raid and asked for reinforcements should Tarleton move in his direction. Parker's small corps of riflemen were operating around the main British base at Portsmouth. Because of the distance from the main armies, Parker's troops had no other force to turn to should they get in a tight spot. Lafayette responded two days later saying he was "much obliged" for the information noting Parker's "situation has been delicate, but you must be sensible, that a reinforcement from this side was impracticable at this juncture. The enemy's command of the water gives them advantages which our expedients cannot counterbalance." He told Parker,

> *"General Wayne and General Morgan, however have crossed and will endeavor to fall in with Tarleton, who, it is said, was to be at Petersburg last night. But this detachment can only be to you a very distant support. I must not flatter you. You must rely, for some time yet, on that circumspection and activity which has heretofore marked the movements of your corps. You are acting the partisan, with a handful of men against a large army, and will, of course, be directed by the principles which govern such corps."*[52]

The Virginians and Continental troops were maneuvered and positioned based on the latest intelligence of Tarleton's movements; news which

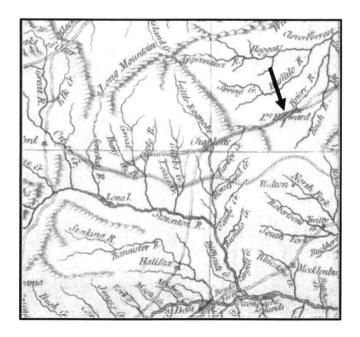

Figure 18 TARLETON'S WESTERN ROUTE – This screenshot from a map illustrating "The marches of Lord Cornwallis in the Southern Provinces, now States of North America; comprehending the two Carolinas, with Virginia and Maryland, and the Delaware counties" depicts Tarleton's route from Prince Edward (arrow) through Charlotte County to Bedford and the return through lower Charlotte County. (Banastre Tarleton's *A History of the Campaigns of 1780 and 1781, in the Southern Provinces of North America.* 1787. Opposite p. 1.Reference: LC Maps of North America, 1750-1789, 1409)

might be exaggerated, misunderstood or consist of pure falsehoods. Over 4,000 militia had been mobilized during the previous months to check the British operations north of the James River. Hundreds of others were serving with Nathanael

Greene in the south. That probably left few men in the Southside counties to respond to Tarleton's raid.

"obliged to scamper"

At least one militia company from Charlotte County moved to stop Tarleton, became isolated and, perhaps dwelling on the atrocity stories involving Tarleton's Legion, decided discretion was the better part of valor.

Harrison Ashworth of Charlotte County was with a militia company mobilized to meet the threat. Ashworth recalled:

> *"Under Captain Jennings, the company marched in the direction of Chinquipin Church in Amelia, but before it reached that place, they understood Tarleton had taken a different route. The militia remained in a state of uncertainty for some time before they could find out the course he had taken. To their surprise, they learned he [Tarleton] had taken a circuitous route by Nottoway and Jennings' Old Ordinary and had reached Prince Edward Court House, cutting them off entirely from the main body of the army [at Amelia]. They then marched directly back, expecting reinforcements everyday but none came. At last the company were ordered to separate, each shifting for himself and to meet again as soon as their personal security would permit."*[53]

James Mullings was in the same company and also declared he had a "distinct recollection" of the march and that Colonel Tarleton "got between them and reinforcements, in consequences of which they were obliged to scamper and escape as they could."[54]

Tarleton departed Prince Edward Court House on the morning of 14 July taking the Cole's Ferry Road towards Charlotte County.[55]

Frances Bland Randolph Tucker, wife of Virginia Militia Lieutenant Colonel St. George Tucker was at her home named 'Bizarre' situated on the Prince Edward-Cumberland County line (near Farmville) and less than eight miles from the British at Prince Edward Court House. She wrote her husband on Saturday night, 14 July stating:

> *"I have been in the utmost distress ever since yesterday – a party of British light Horse consisting of 900 , March'd from [Prince] Edward [Court] House this morning, where they encamped last night; they took the road to Coles Ferry – as it is possible they may return this way, I think I shall set off for someplace of safety on Monday morning. I should have done it before, but I cannot possible get the wheels in tolerable order[.] Til then I am not without an intention of crossing the Potomack, but shall endeavor to stay somewhere on the other side of James River till I hear something more of their rout, or hear something from you which is what I most earnestly wish as I have not had a letter from you since the Engagement at James Town, I am at a loss to know what to do with Hob but I am so apprehensive of the British getting him that I believe I shall take him along with me, indeed, every horse we can get will be necessary for the journey, as we have only one wagon that is very weak, you well know how difficult and arduous my task is, but I shall endeavor to fulfill it with as much cheerfulness*

as I can – Your absence causes my principle pain, for with you I could encounter every hardship, but I must support myself without that comfort & therefore it is needless to mention it. My faithful Servants are every thing I could wish them & are willing to follow my fortune; I shall take with me as Many as will be necessary to assist me on my journey. Tom got here this day from Sappnir[.] He followed the British all the way up, but kept too far in their rear to be discovered; Philis and Hannah are Both well, & the harvest in, as it is at B. Forrest—Tell Beverley I was with Mrs. Randolph yesterday when the alarm came—that she is very well & is at Mr. J. Woodson's[.] Lucy and the rest of the family are well except Jacob & Milly's Child who have the small pox just broke out. I have also heard to day that Mrs. Skipwith & her family have Cross'd James River – Col [Philemon] Holcombe sets of[f] for Camp by day break & says he will deliver you this if he will take the trouble of him, I will send you the Sorrel, I have a letter this day from My Father which I send you as it may possibl[y] be serviceable to my Brother – Mrs. Harleston had determined to stay till your return, but thinks it prudent now to set off –for Philadelphia[.] She begs me to say every thing to you that a friendly heart can dictate – so do the Girls – so do the Boys but we are all too much frightened to be very particular. God Bless My dearest St. George when shall I see him again!...Adieu my Love! Frances Tucker

Our dear little Monkeys are very well & send Papa a kiss."[66]

Tucker was serving with Virginia Militia General Robert Lawson (of Prince Edward) on the north side of the James River at the time and was concerned for the safety of his wife and children. Writing his father-in-law Theodorick Bland on 17 July, Tucker said:

> *"I am much distressed on account of my family, who, I have some reason to fear, may have fallen into the enemy's hands in the excursion, in which they are now engaged, on the south of the James river, from Petersburg upwards. As I can give you no particulars concerning them, I must remain silent on this subject."*[57]

Leaving Prince Edward the British passed through upper Charlotte County on the way to New London. The raiders passed through present day Red House, Wheeler's Springs and McKinney's Old Store. Tarleton's troops traveled on the Ridge Road.[58]

On July 16 the actual route of the British raiders was not known in Richmond. It was feared Tarleton's ride might be an effort to get around Lafayette and strike Richmond from the rear. State Commercial Agent David Ross reported Tarleton was headed to Richmond from the South side of the James and this British threat had kept him in Richmond a few days longer than expected. Ross had reason for concern. He had obtained over 1100 arms plus saddles and tack for 100 horses. The loss of this equipment would have been a tragedy for the American cause.[59]

The mere presence of the British raiders in Virginia's heartland forced the Continental forces to try to save supplies. General Wayne had stores removed in Chesterfield County to a safer place in case Tarleton came that way on his return march. The July 14 order from the Board of War calling out one-seventh of the Southside militia was amended to call out one-fourth of the militia. They were ordered directly to General Greene in the South if Tarleton headed south to take on Greene. Lafayette also authorized the impressments of horses to support a 300 man force of dragoons which he deemed "essentially necessary to prevent further ravages of the enemy." Lafayette also directed the establishment of "dispatch riders; so as to give the earliest and most speedy intelligence of the enemy's movements to the Executive, and to the Commander in Chief in this state."[60]

Tarleton by this time was well through Charlotte and into Bedford (now Campbell) County. Oral tradition suggests Tarleton, in a second attempt to capture Thomas Jefferson, made a dash for *Poplar Forest*, Thomas Jefferson's southern home but Jefferson was not there.[61] There's no primary source information to support this story.

New London was a sizeable town at the time of Tarleton's raid with 80 private homes and several stores. The arsenal consisted of "a long wooden structure used as a magazine, which was kept under guard of soldiers." It was also a point of rendezvous for regional militia. Tarleton reportedly arrived in Bedford County on 16 July. The ammunition factory from Prince Edward had been moved from New London up country while other military supplies were hidden in the town prior to Tarleton getting to the area.⁶² Pension sources say Tarleton did not actually arrive in New London.⁶³

Perhaps these American movements of supplies were unknown to Tarleton as he makes no mention of them. Had he stumbled upon these supplies, it may have been an untimely end. Captain Nathan Reid and 500 Virginia militia men were waiting in ambush for Tarleton in New London. Forewarned of Tarleton's approach, Reid and the others extended themselves to hide supplies and other stores that might be destroyed or stolen by the British raiders. Once the supplies were hidden, they stood guard and waited for the dragoons to show up which they apparently never did.

Wrote Reid later:

> *"I really expected when I heard of Tarleton's being at Prince Edward Court House, that he intended to come as far as this place and I ashure you I never worked more tightly in all my life, than I did for 24 hours…We had but two or three wagons for the most part of the time, and in that case, had no other chance to save the stores, but to hide them in different places round the town, which was done with a great deal of art and security, so that Mr. Tarlton, had he come, I doubt he would have found many of them. The stores [are] all returned to this place without hardly any loss. The men in this county turn'd out, exceeding cleverly, not less than five hundred were collected in two days after the news came, four hundred of which was tolerable well arm'd…Had Mr. Tarlton show'd himself at this place, I am satisfied from the closeness of the woods, and the vast quantity of under growth,*

he must have suffered very considerably."[64]

Tarleton reached the mountains and may have encamped in the area of present day Rustburg, a distance of 55 miles from Prince Edward Court House which would have been a very hard day's ride.

One narrative has Tarleton at the mountains on the 16th of July remaining until the morning of the 18th.[65] A timeline estimate based on period intelligence reports suggests he could have arrived late on the 14th or early morning hours of the 15th and left early on the 16th. Lafayette had reports of Tarleton 32 miles south of Petersburg on the night of the 16th but it is not likely he was that close until late on the 17th or early on the 18th of July.

Greg Eanes

Figure 19 Militia waiting in ambush.

4 THE RETURN TRIP

Tarleton reports resting in Bedford for two days. His men reportedly stole some of the best horses in this area for their own use. While here, Tarleton discovered that Greene "had made no detachment to the northward, but that he was engaged in the siege of Ninety-Six." With this information, Tarleton started back for Suffolk and Cornwallis' main army. In this regard, Tarleton failed to draw off Greene's forces which would have been some relief to British outposts in the South. Tarleton did however keep Greene from being supplied with fresh Virginia militia. Colonel R. Wooding of Halifax County reported that 100 fresh militia slated as relief troops for Greene were not sent due to "the late movements of Col. Tarlton. (sic)"[66]

Tarleton returned through southern Charlotte County reportedly traveling northward on the King's Road (roughly parallel to modern day Rt. 360) passing present day Keysville and through Moore's Ordinary (present day Meherrin). By this time, the colonial response had been made. The 1,300 man American force was concentrated at Goode's Bridge. Wayne's force was positioned on the south side of the Appomattox River in Amelia and ready to do battle.[67]

Lafayette wrote Morgan on July 17 relaying an intelligence report of Tarleton's movements. Lafayette wrote:

> *"My former Intelligences were desisive upon Tarleton's going towards Roenoke [River]. But I just Now Hear that He was last Night at Walker's House Seven Miles above Walker's Mill on Notaway River 32 miles South of Petersburg. He was expected in that town this Night. [General Wayne] is over the [Appomattox] River and Has orders to Be very Cautious But if Tarleton Could Be surprised to Night At Petersburg He is to Make the attempt. I think, My dear friend, we are Rather Scattered and it will Be Better for you to fall Back towards Chesterfield Court House So that if instead of attaking [,][Wayne] was attaked He may Retire to You…I Hardley Believe Tarleton will Come to Petersburg, At all events you May take Such positions in the woods as will effectually Cover you from His Horse. But we are So distant that I leave with you to act according to Circumstances."[68]*

Whether or not this was reliable intelligence or merely a rumor is undetermined however Wayne did, at some point make a movement in Amelia towards Tarleton. Wayne said, "I made a push for Tarleton when he was

Tarleton's Southside Raid

in Amelia; but, obtaining intelligence of my advance he made a precipitate retreat." Because Tarleton moved out of his reach, Wayne concentrated, as ordered by Lafayette, to the south (Amelia County) side of Goode's Bridge.[69]

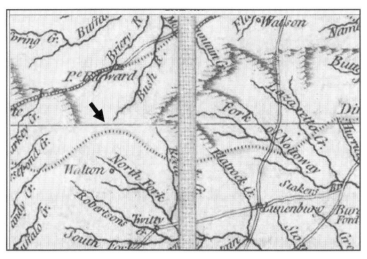

Figure 20 THROUGH LUNENBURG AND NOTTOWAY –
South of Prince Edward, at Moore's Ordinary (now Meherrin; at arrow) on the Lunenburg County line, Tarleton learned of Morgan and Wayne at Goode's Bridge. He burned his wagons and proceeded on a more southerly route through Lunenburg, Brunswick and Nottoway through Dinwiddie, regaining the road at Prince George and proceeded directly to British forces at Portsmouth.

Tarleton learned of the stronger opposition and decided to take a more southerly route on his return trip rather than risk getting trapped or engaging experienced troops in battle. He burned his three wagons and proceeded from Moore's Ordinary, into Lunenburg County, the lower party of Nottoway

County (through present day Blackstone) into Dinwiddie and back through Prince George from a southwesterly direction.

Figure 21 SCHWARTZ'S TAVERN – in Blackstone is believed to have been built prior to the Revolution and was on Tarleton's route of travel. It was purchased by John Schwartz in 1790 who opened it as a tavern in 1798. It is currently open for tours and available for special events.

"grain was destroyed"

Tarleton appears to have ordered a side raid by one element of his force while passing from Charlotte to Lunenburg. One group passed within 30 miles of Taylor's Ferry in Mecklenburg County. There was a commissary and ammunition magazine there at that time. A message from Lafayette to Captain Edmund Gamble sometime prior to July 19 that "the horse of the enemy are in Mecklenburgh near Col. [Lewis] Burwell's...."[70]

This side raid apparently resulted in some bloodshed.

Captain Sam Chapman reported "we have been alarmed here a few days past occasioned by the Enemies cross on this side of the James River. A party of their horse were within 30 miles of Taylor's ferry, on attempting to cross a swamp they were fired upon by a party of our men, on which they retreated with the loss of two officers killed...."[71]

Tarleton's main force continued into Lunenburg County and terrorized the population with their presence. Lunenburg's David Garland reported to Governor Nelson that Tarleton's raiders had done;

> *"considerable damage in destroying the public grain, etc., as also wounding three persons and carrying off some others as Prisoners...He threatens to return immediately after the 16th of next month, when he assures us that he will carry the sword and fire through the land, not sparing any persons but such as hath or may take parole before that time. As there is not one man in twenty that has a gun, etc., in this County (they having at three separate times [been] Impressed into the Countries' Service and not returned), and no army between this and the Enemies Camp at Portsmouth, and only three days march (as Tarleton goes) the people are much alarmed, not knowing what to do, provided Tarleton, or any other of the British forces should come among us. I am apprehensive if that should be the case, the consequences would be disagreeable, as the people would be obliged to submit. This would not be the case if they had arms and ammunition. If there is any to be spared, you'll be a Judge whether it's proper to arm such militia as above described."*

Garland recommended all militia on the south side of the James River be mobilized "to prevent the enemy (in case they should come) going about in small parties to plunder, etc.." Unfortunately, most militias were already overextended.[72]

Lunenburg County militia County Lieutenant N. Hobson reported to Colonel William Davies the loss of grain destined to supply Greene's troops. Wrote Hobson, the "largest magazine of grain was destroyed by Tarleton."[73]

In addition to destruction were threats. Tarleton took prisoners and threatened with captivity anyone who failed to swear allegiance to the King. Most of those captured were paroled. Tarleton put captives on their honor (as was then customary) to cease hostilities until properly (administratively) exchanged for a British soldier. Local citizens had but little choice in the matter; accept parole under threat of death or captivity. The Reverend James Craig of Cumberland Parish, Lunenburg County, was forced to accept parole. The local preacher was said to have been a fire breathing patriot from the earliest days of the Revolution and that his mill was known to be a "storehouse for public provisions" leading Tarleton to target his location and was, reportedly, guided there by a young Tory. As a captive, Rev. Craig was bound by oath to cease his preaching in support of the patriot cause. His mill on Flat Rock Creek was burned to the ground but not before barrels of flour were rolled into the mill pond and creek. Afterwards it was reported the British made Rev. Craig slaughter and cook his own hogs and mutton to feed the same British dragoons who burned his mill. They also reportedly fed his corn to their horses. It is said that after Tarleton left, the flour barrels were retrieved from the water and upon inspection, it was found that the outside of the flour had become wet and formed a protective barrier thus saving most of the flour on the inside of the protective layers. While most citizens considered Tarleton's paroles non-binding because of the circumstances, the preacher kept his word and refused to preach, much to the frustration of his congregation. So much so that 99 local citizens signed a petition to Governor Thomas Nelson urging him to formally 'exchange' Rev. Craig with an appropriate British counterpart, so the Reverend could once again resume his pulpit and articulate advocacy of the revolution.[74]

Another version of this story, repeated in Howe's *History*, suggests Rev. Craig was the one responsible for rolling the barrels of flour into the mill pond in order to save them. He was reportedly in the act of rolling the last barrel into the water when Tarleton appeared. According the local Lunenburg historian Landon C. Bell, "Howe's account accords with the tradition of the county" where Bell remembered hearing it as a child in the 1800s. Bell said, "If Tarleton had discovered the flour and had attempted to destroy it, he probably would not have endeavored to do so by rolling the barrels in the mill pond. Such would have been an ineffective measure, for the water would only strike into the flour a short distance, the residue remaining perfectly good."[75]

The Rev. Craig had been the local minister since 1759 and would remain in place until his death in 1795. He also practiced medicine.[76]

Passing back through Nottoway Parrish the raiders stopped in the community that would become known as Black's and White's and later Blackstone. Tradition has it they visited a tavern before moving another two miles to Edmondson's Old Ordinary which was also burned. Tarleton's men burned a grain quarters to the ground. The area became known as "Burnt Quarter" or "Burnt Ordinary." It later became known as Morganville[77] Based on documented events, it is likely the raiders backtracked slightly and took a southerly route to Brunswick rather than the more direct route to Petersburg, possibly to avoid American soldiers.

Brunswick militia Colonel John Jones reported to Governor Nelson that he had 600 militia but only 50 guns. Hardly enough for a pitched battle against the raiders. Jones said the British "distressed the inhabitants greatly." Some of the raiders reportedly crossed the Nottoway River at a place later named Cutbank and traveled to Smokey Ordinary, an inn on the stage road between Petersburg and North Carolina. They remained about two days. Before leaving they set fire to tobacco warehouses at the place. The fire reportedly smoldered creating a heavy smoke for several days leading local citizens to call the place Smokey Ordinary. Tarleton's men also searched the village for a British Army deserter before leaving. The deserter was hidden in a bed by a girl servant. He was placed sideways "under the cover of a bolster"[2] and when British soldiers searching the place prodded

---

[2] **A 'bolster' is described as a long thick pillow, placed under other pillows for support.**

the mattress with swords and bayonets, they missed stabbing the deserter who successfully hid.[78]

Tarleton passed through Prince George County on the main road to Petersburg. While in Prince George his raiders reportedly burned the court house. One source says, "the courthouse and its contents were put to flames and irreplaceable records were either destroyed or carried off."[79]

Passing through neighboring Sussex the raiders apparently visited one Augustine Claiborne who later said Tarleton "and his gang of thieves" stole "six valuable nags." He was upset because he had already furnished the American army with two of his best horses.[80]

Nine months later Claiborne reported he was left without any horses but that Tarleton left a "pretty valuable gelding" which Claiborne described as "quite run down." He said he had cared for this particular horse, had fattened it up and had taken steps necessary to see that its owner recovered it but to no avail. In March 1782 the Virginia Militia Quartermasters seized the horse as contraband of war but told Claiborne they would leave it if ordered by their state commander.[81]

North Carolina's Response
North Carolina Governor Thomas Burke had only recently been elected by the time of Tarleton's Southside Raid. A native of Galway, Ireland, he immigrated to Norfolk, Virginia and lived in that area before moving his family to Hillsborough, North Carolina in 1772 where he practiced law and worked a

plantation. At about age 30, a member of North Carolina's Provincial Congress of 1776, Burke was on the committee that investigated British outrages against the American colonies which authorized North Carolina's representatives at the Second Continental Congress in Philadelphia to vote for independence. He was an early and ardent Revolutionary giving freely of his own wealth and property to support the war effort.

Burke became governor in June 1781 and faced extraordinary challenges with a nearly all-out civil war between North Carolina Loyalists and Patriot militias. Burke sought to impose order while also trying to support the larger war effort by funneling supplies and troops to Nathanael Greene in the south and taking precautionary measures because of the threat Cornwallis posed from the north.[82]

Virginia militia Lieutenant Colonel John Bannister, then a member of the Virginia House of Delegates from Petersburg, sent Burke a letter, dated 8 July saying, "The enemy are at Surry Court House perhaps on their way to South Quay but this is uncertain for you know how difficult it is to enter into the designs of our enemy."[83]

Virginia militia Colonel and Tidewater area Partisan leader Josiah Parker wrote to Burke and Nathanael Greene on 14 July from his camp in Isle of Wight County. He said:

> *"When I wrote you last, I was not certain [Banastre] Tarleton had advanced up the country & proceeded towards Hillsborough. On Monday last, he left*

Petersburg, took the Hillsborough route and I fear before this reaches you, he will be there. I have directed the Express to proceed with Expadetion (sic) in order that you may apprise Gen. Greene. Tarleton's force is 700…".[84]

Continental Line Southern Department Deputy Quartermaster General Colonel Nicholas Long in Halifax was in receipt of a similar letter from Parker. He notifies North Carolina militia General Allen Jones in nearby Northampton County and recommends Greene be notified of this potential threat from the north. Jones was also on the 'Council of the Extraordinary', a group of three men designated to help the Governor run the war in North Carolina.[85]

On 17 July Continental Lt. Col. Henry Dixon of Caswell County sent a letter to Colonel Long advising of news from Lafayette who said the British had evacuated Williamsburg, marched to Jamestown and intend to send part of their soldiers to besieged New York while the rest garrison Portsmouth. Dixon added,

"but from their number of cavalry he [Lafayette] rather imagines they will push to the Southward. It is therefor of the highest importance that Genl. Greene's orders be immediately carried into execution relating to the removal of the Stores to Moravian Town, and that all valuable horses, Beef Cattle, etc., etc., be moved from the Road leading from James Town on [the] James River to Campbellton on Cap[e] Fear. Also on the road leading to Harrisburg to Salisbury, etc. I have [written] to Governor Burke

> *informing him of this order and should he not approve of its being executed He will inform you so immediately.*[86]

The warnings alarmed Burke. His Hillsborough home was only about 40 miles south of the Dan River and the Virginia border and on one of the main roads running to Virginia. A British force of 700 mounted men could move fast through the state, destroy supplies, encourage local Tories and threaten Nathanael Greene's Continentals in South Carolina. Action must be taken to stop or at least impede any British movements south. Burke mobilized militia forces all along the Virginia-North Carolina border.

On 18 July Burke issued an order mobilizing Colonel Francis Locke's Salisbury District. He wrote:

> *"...movements of the Enemy in Virginia seem to threaten us with a rapid march of a body of Horse through this state. I request you therefore to collect as many riflemen as you can from the draught [draft] to have raised [for] Gen. Greene…if they have not already marched and order them under the active …of your officers to move on to the crossing places on Dan and Staunton Rivers, in order that we may take advantage of these [sections]. If the draughts have already marched, I beg you will call out as many good riflemen as you can from the counties in your district and direct them to march towards the above mentioned rivers as fast as possible. The service which they can render may be very essential and the time they may be out must be short, however they shall have credit for it on a future tour…Should the*

> *Enemy move towards the above waters I will come up to meet your men and dispute the passes with them. Should they attempt crossing lower down, I will send up for you and ...let me beg of you sir, and every friend to his country, to be diligent and, if possible let us check those savages."*

He further advised that if the enemy did not show, the men would be sent to Greene. He did not anticipate more than one month service for the militia.[87]

A similar letter was sent to General John Butler commanding the Hillsborough District militia (six counties). Burke requested the commanding officers of the border counties of Orange, Granville and Caswell counties "to collect all the riflemen in their respective counties" and concentrate them at select river crossings. The Orange and Caswell riflemen were to defend Taylor's Ferry on the Dan River while the Granville men[88] were to defend Kemp's Ferry on the Roanoke River. He further directed that "measures should be taken to supply ammunition and provisions" to the men.[89] About one-half mile from Taylor's Ferry was a militia powder magazine.[90]

Similar orders were sent to the commanding officers of militia in Franklin and Warren Counties (formerly Bute County) with their riflemen to assemble at Burton's Ferry on the Roanoke River. Burke said, "to prevent those savages from penetrating our country is of the highest importance."[91]

After taking the necessary steps to mobilize the North Carolina border militia, Burke wrote and dispatched a circular letter to the six southern Virginia counties that bordered North Carolina, specifically to the commanding officers of militia in Brunswick, Mecklenburg, Halifax, Charlotte, Pittsylvania and Henry Counties. He advised the Virginians that Tarleton would likely attempt a crossing into North Carolina with the intent to travel to South Carolina where Greene's Continentals were currently operating. Burke advised the Virginians of his actions mobilizing militia at the various Ferry Crossings "in order to dispute them with the enemy". He requested the Virginia militia companies cooperate with his men on those routes and locations and "to keep out people who can give regular notice of the enemy's movements and to communicate with me at Nuttbush in Granville County all the intelligence you can collect in order that I may take the most effectual measures for counteracting the designs of the Enemy."[92]

After concentrating militia forces on the primary lanes of travel Burke sent a message to Nathanael Greene summarizing the intelligence he had received, giving his assessment of the military situation. Burke wrote,

> *"Colonel Parker is probably mistaken in his conjecture both as to the object and rout of the Enemy. The last intelligence I can procure is as follows. Col. Tarlton (sic) with 700 or 800 cavalry and mounted infantry penetrated through Amelia to Prince Edward. Burned Mr. Daniel Jones' Mill in the former destroyed Stores, etc., in the latter. Then the force divided, one division penetrating through Powhatan and wheeling to the right through Chesterfield intending on joining the enemy at or near*

> *Petersburg when Lord Cornwallis was about the latter end of the last work. The other division proceeded through Lunenburg and Charlotte where they were opposed by a small party of militia who took a Lieutenant and some privates prisoner. They then retreated along [the] Meherrin River and, in their way burned a Mr. Craig's Mill. The evening before last they were seen near Lamb's on the Petersburg Road and it is supposed they encamped there. Their route seemed to be directed for Hick's Ford. I am apprehensive lest their intentions might be to surprise Col. Parker, who by his letter seems to have no expectation of their near approach to him."*

Burke advised of his own readiness to engage Tarleton if the British moved south.[93] While the reported information is not totally accurate, it was Burke's on-scene assessment based on various reports. He had to make judgments as he interpreted the information. Burke's mobilization and coordinating actions illustrate a man capable of strategic analysis and strategic leadership. His willingness to command at the front also demonstrates a level of moral courage.

In Nuttbush on the 19th, Burke wrote Virginia Governor Thomas Nelson noting,

> *"The excursion of the enemy through your counties to the Southward of James River & so far west as Charlotte have somewhat alarmed us. Their burning mills and other part of their proceedings indicate that they are sensible of their inferiority & want to procure safety by making the subsistence of our armies difficult and precarious"*

Burke speculated that if Cornwallis went to New York, as had been reported, his cavalry would like strike for South Carolina. Burke said,

> *"That I might, however, make every attempt possible against the enemy, I have ordered all our riflemen from the several counties…to march toward the passes on [Staunton], Dan and Roanoke [Rivers] in order that if his lordship's cavalry [meet] them, we may give them some opposition."*

Burke also suggested a line of couriers be established so he and Nelson could communicate directly and coordinate military activities.[94]

Elsewhere in Virginia

On 19 July the Governor authorized the formation of a force of 200 dragoons to be raised in the Southside Virginia counties of Lunenburg, Mecklenburg, Charlotte, Prince Edward, Pittsylvania and Bedford. The action appears to be a late attempt to establish a local reaction force to such raids as Tarleton's.[95]

General Washington, commanding the Main Army in the north, made note of Tarleton's raid in a diary entry. He wrote, "A letter from Marquis de la Fayette informed me that after Lord Cornwallis had crossed the James River he detached Tarleton with a body of horse into Amelia County with a view, as was supposed, to destroy some stores which had been deposited there, but which had been previously removed."[96]

On July 20th, Lord Cornwallis was in Suffolk still awaiting Tarleton's return. He advised General Alexander Leslie, then in New York with Sir Henry Clinton, that he could not move to a position on the coast until Tarleton joined him.[97]

Cornwallis left a detachment at Suffolk to meet Tarleton on his return and guide his force to Portsmouth. Before Tarleton reached that place his force passed through Isle of Wight County where the raiders struck at Smithfield but not before the public records were saved by Mrs. Francis Young, the wife of the Deputy Clerk of the Court. Mr. Young was an officer in the Revolutionary Army and on duty with his unit at the time of the raid. It is reported Mrs. Young "removed the records to a farm near Smithfield where they were buried in a 'hair trunk', which is still [1934] in possession of her descendants. The records remained buried until after the surrender at Yorktown and when the trunk was opened they [the records] were found in a good state of preservation with the exception of the 'Great Book' which had been damaged by worms."[98]

The raiders then passed through the community of Benn's Church. About seven miles away was Macclesfield, the home of partisan leader Colonel Josiah Parker. Tarleton's troop unsuccessfully raided the home in an effort to capture Parker. Parker had been there but escaped in time. Parker wrote, "According to custom, with the assistance of good heels and a severe retrograde I escaped Tarleton having good intelligence on his movements." They continued on through the village of Chuckatuck arriving in Suffolk on July 24, 1781.[99] The Southside Virginia raid was over.

Tarleton's men joined up with the British raiding party that had burned South Quay on the Blackwater River in Southampton County earlier on July 16. Together they entered the main British camp at Portsmouth. They soon deployed to Yorktown and Gloucester.[100]

5 THE FALLOUT

Regardless of Tarleton's toll, the repercussions of the raid continued for some time after it ended. On July 22 Wayne, still at Goode's Bridge, wrote to Lafayette telling him he had heard of the arrival of transports at Portsmouth. He said the transports were insufficient for use by horses and suggested the British concentrated at Portsmouth would either strike towards the south to take on Greene or launch a raid north on the Potomac River to threaten coastal positions. In either case, he suggested Tarleton would reinforce the British in the south. With this in mind, Wayne sought orders.[101]

A few days later, Wayne wrote to Virginia Governor Thomas Nelson advising that he would respond to any British threat when he becomes aware of them. Wayne emphasized the need for intelligence before he could counter the threat. Wayne wrote, "should the enemy make a forward move into the country or continue marauding I will at all events advance to push them, or cover the inhabitants from the depredations of such cailiffs. I shall therefore wish the earliest intelligence of any move that they have, or are about to make."[102]

On July 22, Captain Brown Price, Commander of Military Stores at New London wrote to Major John Pryor advising he was staying put in his present position though he had learned of Tarleton's return "down country." He said he was staying in place because of the "great expense of hiring wagons to move stores." Price said he had all the material and put the men to work. He said the supplies were not damaged by the weather and noted nothing was lost with the exception of a few swords and about forty pounds of gunpowder "owing to the barrels giving way when removed."

Price wanted to know if the ammunition lab then at Irvin's under Captain Bohannon was to be moved and if so, where? He added the "men needed money, have none...can get no credit in this part of the world" though he had used every persuasive method he could. He alluded the place was so poor and destitute that "Captain Grice is not able to buy himself a chicken."[103]

Figure 22 Thomas Nelson, Jr.

Apparently the lab was to remain in place. On July 23 Major Pryor wrote Col. Davies saying he had sent men, powder, paper and lead to the lab at Irvin's in response to Capt. Bohannon's request. He also said he would send arms to that location which apparently was considered the safest place from British raids.[104]

Virginia Governor Thomas Nelson even entered into a correspondence with Cornwallis in an effort to recoup some of the damages to private property inflicted by Tarleton's raiders and get some of the American prisoners paroled. On July 23 Nelson wanted to know whether any restitution would be made for slaves and other property. He also asked that Cornwallis free former Col. William Archer and a "Mr. Royall of Amelia County, captured by Tarleton's troops for no apparent cause." Nelson said, Archer "is of an age which exempt him from military duty; the latter bears no other character than that of a citizen of the state. As I cannot suppose that your Lordship regards such persons as the objects of hostile treatment, I flatter myself you will on this representation have them immediately restored to their liberty."[105]

Colonel Parker wrote on July 24 telling of his near escape, adding, "On his way down he [Tarleton] had a skirmish…The event of which was Tarleton lost one way or another near 40 men besides horses. He got yesterday to Suffolk where the British rear remained last night."[106]

On July 27 Nelson wrote to George Washington and reported,:

"Tarleton, by sudden incursions into those parts of the country that he knew were not in arms, has collected a number of horses, that have enabled him to run about, paroling citizens, whom he has taken in their beds. Whenever a force sufficient to oppose them has been collected, they have always retreated immediately. It is certain they have done much injury both private & public, but I have this consolation, that they are further from making a conquest of the State than when they enter'd it. I do not believe ten Men have join'd them. They have made Whigs of Tories."[107]

Cornwallis replied to Nelson on August 6 from Yorktown saying he made no order to capture of slaves but many have come with him. He said that owners, under certain unspecified conditions, could come to the British camp to search for their slaves and horses and take them home. He said he already ordered the release of such people as Archer and Royall.[108]

On August 14 Cornwallis ordered his deputy Charles O'Hara to release the American militiamen captured before June 18. He also ordered, "I would have all those taken by Tarleton dismissed on parole, unless some particular crime is alleged against them. I would have you detain all prisoners charged with heinous offenses and the very violent people of Princess Anne and the neighborhood of Portsmouth who may be some security to those who have been more favorable to us."[109]

On September 3 Nelson wrote another letter advising Cornwallis that Archer and Royall were still held "on a prison ship" and asked for their release.[110]

Cornwallis responded on September 8th. He wrote Nelson, "When I left Portsmouth I gave directions to release all prisoners who had not been taken in arms or who were not remarkable for persecuting their countrymen of different political opinions; and when I answered your former leter (sic), I thought it probable the Mssrs. Ryell (sic) and Archer had been released as not coming under either of those descriptions. But I having [been] apprised [by] the commanding officer [Tarleton] at Portsmouth that those gentlemen were made prisoners not only for refusing to give their own paroles but because they had threatened to force their neighbors [who had given paroles] to break them, he thought proper to detain them; And for the same reasons I find myself under the necessity of retaining them in confinement."[111]

On September 15 Cornwallis ordered the release of both men due to their age and infirmities however it was too late. Archer contracted smallpox and died while a prisoner in Portsmouth.[112]

A little more than a month later Tarleton surrendered with Cornwallis at Yorktown on October 19, 1781. Also surrendered were 192 men of his British Legion.[113]

Summary

In just fifteen days, Tarleton's small raiding party covered over 400 miles unchecked by any large patriot force. Though not a failure, the raid was hardly the success the British wanted. Wrote Tarleton later:

> *"The stores destroyed, either of a public or private nature, were not in quantity or value equivalent to the damage sustained in the skirmishes on the route, and the loss of men and horse by the excessive heat of the climate. The intelligence which occasioned this march was exceedingly imperfect; The stores, which were the principal object of the expedition, had been conveyed from Prince Edward Court House, and all that quarter of the country to Hillsborough [NC] and General Greene's army, upwards of a month before the British light troops commenced their move."[114]*

Tarleton does not provide a casualty list but his narrative implies there were skirmishes other than Francisco's fight at Ward's Tavern, the incident near Briery Creek and the one near Taylor's Ferry. These other actions may have been nothing more than sniping or bushwhacking by country militia determined to take some small toll on the raiders. Lafayette referred to Tarleton's casualties in a letter to Anthony Wayne on July 25. The Maquis wrote, "Pray, find out who Tarleton Has Been fighting with Below Petersburg – for fighting He Has Been! – and My flag dragoon Saw His wounded. He Adds that on Hearing we Had Crossed the [Appomattox] River [at Goode's Bridge] Tarleton Burnt His Waggons." Lafayette likewise reported to Washington that "on his precipitate return from Amelia County Colonel Tarleton suffered some loss from militia light parties." Parker likewise notes a significant skirmish as does Burke whose narrative suggests the action may have taken place in Charlotte County. Based on the documented incidents, Tarleton may have lost as many as four or five killed in action, two wounded and prisoners of war that included a Lieutenant and several privates.

Lafayette tells of an officer of Tarleton's Legion that was taken prisoner and interrogated for military information. He wrote, "an officer of Tarleton's Legion who Has Been taken was Brought to My Quarters. He had much Conversation with My aids de Camp, and Being an Unguarded Young Man Spoke very freely. He Says Lord Cornwallis and Colonel Tarleton are Certainly Going to Newyork. He Adds

the Light Infantry and a Regiment of Horse Do
Certainly Embark for Maneuvres through Virginia.
He thinks the Guards are to Remain Here—Does not
know the Dispositions of Any other troops. I thought
this was worth Mentioning to your – Would to God
this Embarkation Could Be Intercepted!"[115]

Tarleton never realized the military impact of his raid.
Based on the evidence, Tarleton's little band of about
300 raiders effectively tied up over 2,000 and possibly
3,000 American soldiers preventing them from
performing other duties. This includes over 1,300
men at Goode's Bridge, the estimated 500 militia at
Bedford, about 100 militia from Halifax County,
Virginia plus hundreds of others moving stores and
guarding river crossings to include those militia in
upper North Carolina mobilized by that state's
governor. In other words, the American troops were
"fixed in place" because of the threat posed by
Tarleton's British Legion.

The raid likewise disrupted the manufacture of war
materials. Because the ammunition laboratories were
being moved, they were effectively shut down and
inoperative for a couple of weeks until it was deemed
safe to re-establish operations. The evidence suggests
a major effort was made in many quarters to move
supplies, at least some of which was lost due to the
movement. The massive transfer of supplies and
equipment was time consuming, involved manpower
and the use of valuable horses and wagons that may
have been needed elsewhere such as for transporting
supplies to the various Armies in the field. The
response of the militia to moving and protecting these

industries does justice to an organization maligned by some historians of this period. Militia efforts may well have also saved an iron factory from destruction. In a sense, this was the great American success in the raid and comparable to the actions of Civil War partisan Col. John S. Mosby's Rangers when Sheridan brought destruction into the Shenandoah Valley. At that time, Mosby's Rangers were likewise fully occupied moving important supplies rather than engaging in small unit combat operations.[116]

Tarleton's raid also disrupted the manufacture of foodstuffs though to what extent cannot be determined. At least two mills were record as having been destroyed. These were Daniel Jones Mill in Amelia and the Flat Rock Creek (Craig's) Mill in Lunenburg. Granaries in Mannboro (Amelia), Lunenburg, and Dinwiddie were destroyed along with an estimated 600-700 bushels of wheat in Amelia.

An undetermined quantity of tobacco was also reportedly burned thereby having an economic impact. Tobacco, Virginia's money crop, was used for trade and foreign credit.

Coupled with the practical damage was the psychological impact on the populace. Up to this point the citizens of Virginia's interior had been untouched by active combat. They were now faced with war on their front doorstep. The great concern of the civilian population against further incursions is reflected in the letters to Governor Thomas Nelson, many of which call for arms or protection for fear Tarleton might return. The counties were destitute of arms because of state demands for guns made the previous February when large numbers of Virginia militia were being equipped to aid Greene. At that time many citizens gave up personal weapons for use by the government. Most of these weapons were lost or abandoned resulting in an unarmed militia that was combat ineffective for want of arms when Tarleton's raid occurred.[117]

Details on American casualties are likewise sketchy. Several prominent citizens were taken prisoner. Three men are reported to have been wounded in Lunenburg. The only identifiable American death is Amelia militia Colonel William Archer who died of smallpox while a prisoner of the British.

Tarleton's raid cannot be deemed a failure when one looks at the results in the context of a stand-alone military operation. While the British Legion failed to draw Greene's army north, it was successful in immobilizing a significant portion of the American militia in Virginia and North Carolina, destroyed a quantity of stores, disrupted the manufacture of arms and created a psychological impact locally.

With this in mind though, the raid had no impact on the overall British war effort. The initial Allied movements of the Yorktown Campaign were set in motion while the raid was in progress. There was nothing Tarleton could do to stop what Lafayette would call 'the fifth act' in the great play called the American Revolution.

End

Greg Eanes

Annex A

Logistics Targets
Quartermaster Department - Virginia

Pursuant to a January 1, 1781 order from General Edward Carrington, Deputy Quarter Master General for the Southern (Continental) Army, the quartermaster department in Virginia was reorganized into nine primary districts in the eastern portion of the state, each with a deputy quartermaster in charge.

These included the Districts of Alexandria, Fredericksburg, Richmond, Petersburg, Williamsburg, Prince Edward, the Rivers (Staunton and Dan), Charlottesville and Carter's Ferry. The District of Prince Edward was formed in February 1781. By April 1781 the District of Charlottesville was eliminated when Culpeper was incorporated into Fredericksburg and the remaining counties (Albemarle, Orange, Fluvanna, Amherst and Augusta) were merged into the Carter's Ferry District.

There generally was a principal post in each district. Principal posts or depots were established at the following places: Alexandria, Fredericksburg, Carter's Ferry, Richmond ("where the principal factories for the Southern Department are established"), Williamsburg, Charlottesville, (principal post for the accommodation of the Convention Troops), Winchester ("where good wagons and horses may be procured with great ease") and Petersburg.

Charlottesville was discontinued as a principal post in April 1781 when the British Convention prisoners were moved to Winchester.

Within each district were "depend posts" which collected supplies in each county. Each was governed by a Storekeeper. There appears to have been several 'supporting posts' within each county. Counties had several appointed Commissary officers charged with collecting supplies in their respective communities. Supplies were stored in warehouses and public granaries. When supplies were needed the quartermasters would direct shipments from smaller posts to a central location, a "principal post" or directly to the army in the field. If supplies were not in stock, each local commissary would attempt to raise his levy by visiting local citizens.

Transportation between posts was made by public or private wagons drafted for the purpose. Wagons would transport supplies to the next post where supplies were offloaded for movement to the next link in the chain. Conceptually, this meant that less time was involved in transporting supplies and placed less of a burden on private citizens who may have had a wagon levied or who may have been drafted for a militia tour to move supplies.

Such an extended system of supply provided numerous economic and logistics targets. The flow of supplies could be temporarily disrupted by the appearance of raiders such as the British Legion but the system could not be destroyed because there were so many minor depots spread out across a vast area.

Tarleton appears to have bypassed some of these such as the depot at Hendersonville in what is now Nottoway County as well as a significant target near Taylor's Ferry in Mecklenburg County.

Every male citizen between the ages of 16 and 50 were members of the militia therefore available for activation. Thomas Jefferson, as Governor, estimated Virginia had an estimated 45,000 militia men. Numerous pension claims reflect men were often activated to perform "routine" duties such as guarding supplies or less routine duties of moving supplies out of harm's way due to the threat of a British raid.

Sources: Calendar of Virginia State Papers, Vol. 2 p157-169; *Amelia County Order Book 1782;* **Dorman's Revolutionary War Pensions** and *Virginia Publick Service Claims.*

Greg Eanes

Annex B Calendar for July 1781

```
July 1781


Gregorian

  S   M  Tu   W  Th   F   S
  1   2   3   4   5   6   7
  8   9  10  11  12  13  14
 15  16  17  18  19  20  21
 22  23  24  25  26  27  28
 29  30  31
```

Source: www.hf.rim.or.jp

Greg Eanes

Annex C
--- *An Auto Tour* ---
Tarleton's Southside Raid

Heritage Driving Tours have proven to be critical to developing the tourism infrastructure of rural communities and they are beneficial to heritage tourists. In rural areas much of the original landscape remains untouched by time.

There are no less than 43 Virginia Department of Historic Resources Highway Makers mentioning Banastre Tarleton and 24 are related to his Southside Raid with nine giving details on local incidents and 15 being 'County' markers merely noting Tarleton 'passed this way' on a raid. Unfortunately none of these have been tied together to form a Virginia Revolutionary War Heritage Tourism trail similar to the Virginia Civil War Heritage Tourism trails.

While roads have been renamed, redirected or widened, a significant portion of Tarleton's route, with the exception of hard surfacing, remains as it was at the time of the American Revolution. This is particularly true for many portions through the Southside Virginia counties of Amelia, Nottoway, Prince Edward, Charlotte, Campbell and Lunenburg. Elements of the original roadbed are still used by modern day commuters, most unaware of the historical significance of their back-country trace.

What follows are annotated Virginia Highway Maps highlighting stops made by Tarleton and illustrating how these may be reached today by car.

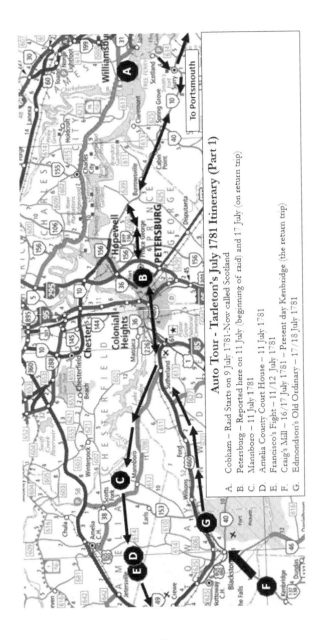

Tarleton's Southside Raid

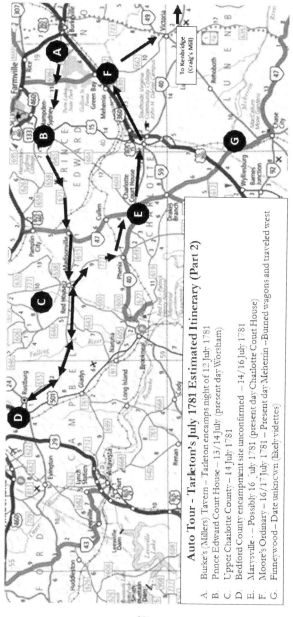

Auto Tour - Tarleton's July 1781 Estimated Itinerary (Part 2)

A. Burke's (Miller's) Tavern – Tarleton encamps night of 12 July 1781
B. Prince Edward Court House – 13/14 July (present day Worsham)
C. Upper Charlotte County – 14 July 1781
D. Bedford County encampment site unconfirmed – 14/16 July 1781
E. Marysville – Possibly 16 July 1781 (present day Charlotte Court House)
F. Moore's Ordinary – 16/17 July 1781 – Present day Meherrin – Burned wagons and traveled west
G. Finneywood – Date unknown (likely videttes)

Annex D
Peter Francisco

As a small boy of about five years of age, Peter Francisco was kidnapped from his native Portugal (the Azores), taken to Virginia and abandoned on June 23, 1765 on a wharf at City Point (now Hopewell, Va).

He spoke no English and kept repeating the name "Pedro Francisco". His shoes had silver buckles with the initials "P.F." His dark complexion suggested he was a native of Italy or the Iberian Peninsula. He was provided a bed in a warehouse and local women took turns feeding him until Prince George County authorities had him placed in a County 'poor house'.

Judge Anthony Winston, an uncle of Patrick Henry, learned of the boy and adopted him, taking him to 'Hunting Tower Plantation' in Buckingham County where Peter worked as an indentured servant in the fields and blacksmith shop. By the age 15 he was said to have grown to six feet, six inches tall and weighed in at 260 pounds.

Judge Winston was an active revolutionary and hosted meetings at his house. He took Peter to Richmond to a House of Burgesses meeting at St. John's Church where Peter heard Patrick Henry's famous 'Liberty or Death' speech.

In December 1776, at the age of 16, Peter was allowed to enlist in the 10th Virginia Continental Line. He served with distinction with Washington's Army in the north at Brandywine, Germantown, Monmouth and was a volunteer for the 20-man 'forlorn hope' that spearheaded the attack on Stony Point. In the latter event, one eyewitness said Francisco,

> *"was the second man who entered the fort and distinguished himself by numerous acts of bravery and intrepidity—in a charge which was ordered to be made around the flag staff, he killed three British grenadiers and was the first man who laid hold of the flagstaff and being badly wounded laid on it that*

night and in the morning delivered it to [Lieutenant] Colonel [Francois-Louis Teissedre de] Fleury."[3]

He reportedly also served for a period as one of Washington's personal guard. Washington presented Francisco with a sword that fit his size. It was six feet long and had a five foot blade.

Returning home after his service as a Continental Regular, Peter was engaged in the Virginia Militia under a Colonel William Mayo of Powhatan. He was at the battle of Camden, SC (16 August 1780) where he saved the life of Colonel Mayo by giving a British assailant 'buck and ball' before he could bayonet the Colonel. He also gave the Colonel a British horse on which to escape. After seeing a cannon abandoned because the trail horses had been killed, Francisco took the time to loosen the 1,100 pound tube, placed it on his shoulders and carried it off for future American use. By the time of the Battle of Guilford Courthouse, Francisco was with the Prince Edward militia cavalry attached to William Washington's dragoons. Using his now famous sword, Francisco eliminated eleven British troops. At one point his leg was pinned to his horse by a British bayonet thrust with Francisco quickly dispatching his attacker. He was struck by

---

[3] **Statement of Captain William Evans. Colonel Fleury (1749-1799)** led one of three attacking columns in the 16 July 1779 battle of Stony Point and was reportedly the first man in the British upper works with Francisco close behind. Another source says a 'Major Gibbon' was the first man. The battle started after midnight and the upper works were captured about 25 minutes after it was assaulted with the entire attack taking about one hour. General "Mad Anthony" Wayne commanded the overall assault.

British grapeshot, was severely wounded and left for dead on the battlefield. A Quaker found him and provided care.

He was still recovering from wounds when Tarleton's Raiders struck Southside leading to his recall with other militia, his reconnaissance mission and the incident at Ward's Tavern.

Francisco, at age 21, was also at Yorktown serving with other Virginians under the Marquis de Lafayette. He survived the war having participated in many battles and having been wounded multiple times.

In the post-war period he married several times (losing his wife on each occasion) and lived in Cumberland, Charlotte, Prince Edward and Buckingham Counties at various intervals. In time he was elected Sergeant of Arms for the Virginia House of Delegates dying of appendicitis in January 1836. He was buried with full military honors in Shockoe Hill Cemetery in Richmond.

To this day, the Society of the Descendants of Peter Francisco works to keep his memory alive. [4]

Figure 23 Peter Francisco's Signature

---

[4] Visit http://www.peterfrancisco.org/aboutus.php

Virginia's Peter Francisco Day was officially designated as March 15 by Governor Linwood Holton in 1973.

PETER FRANCISCO DAY PROCLAIMED --- Governor Linwood Holton has proclaimed March 15 as Peter Francisco Day in Virginia. The signing of the proclamation, last Wednesday, Feb. 17, in the state capitol, was witnessed by several local citizens who have been instrumental in efforts to have Francisco recognized by the state. Pictured above with Gov. Holton at the signing are, left to right, Mrs. H.J. Fay of Crewe, Mrs. Julia Budwell Barber of Crewe, Miss M.J. Jefferson of Amelia, Mrs. Hallie N. Richmond, Bill Willis of Crewe, Mrs. Bessie Hawks of Crewe, Town Manager C. A. Riser of Crewe, Mrs. Alice Jones of Richmond, Miss Lisa Queensberry of Crewe, Mrs. Elizabeth Fray of Richmond, son, an instructor

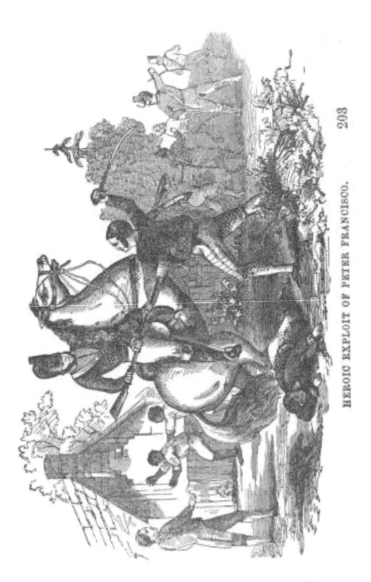

Figure 24 From the 1854 issue of The Battle-fields of the Revolution by Thomas Y. Rhoads

Figure 25 Drawing from <u>Illustrated American Advertiser: The Historical Picture Gallery</u>, Vol. 5 (1856) by Jno. R. Chapin

Greg Eanes

Bibliography

Manuscripts

Burke, Thomas. *Thomas Burke Papers, 1763-1852.* Collection 00104. Wilson Library. University of North Carolina at Chapel Hill. Burke was the Governor of North Carolina.

Cornwallis, Charles (The Earl). *Cornwallis Papers. Correspondence from Earl Cornwallis.* Letters to General Clinton and other Officers. Public Record Office papers containing correspondence related to Cornwallis' and other British military operations during the American War for Independence. Part of the Virginia Colonial Records Project accessed through the Library of Virginia.

Cornwallis, Charles (The Earl). *Cornwallis Papers. Original Correspondence and Military Despatches.* July to November 1781. Public Record Office papers containing official correspondence from Cornwallis to various parties. Contains some general troop returns. Part of the Virginia Colonial Records Project accessed through the Library of Virginia.

Damerel, John E. (compiler). Personal Papers Collection: *Campaign of 1781: Tarleton's Raid, 1973.* Damerel worked with Elie Weeks of the Virginia Bicentennial Commission to prepare a map of Revolutionary War military operations in Virginia. These papers consist of extensive correspondence as individuals try to piece together the exact route of Tarleton's Raid.

Innes, Harry. Papers. *Commissary Papers, May 1781-February 1782*. Bedford County Escheator's Papers. 28 Volumes. Six boxes. Library of Congress collection. Bedford County was the farthest point of Tarleton's Raid and the place where Prince Edward County supplies were moved for safety.

Morton, John. *Papers*. Deputy Commissary in Prince Edward County. 1780-1782. One volume of papers. Library of Congress collection. Prince Edward was a designated point for collection of war materials.

Order Book, Amelia County, Virginia 1781-1782. The Amelia County Order Book is the official record of transactions of the County representatives, militia officers, road surveyors, criminal court actions and petitions before government such as petitions for payment for services rendered on behalf of the Revolution. These were known as public service claims.

Steuben, Friedrich Wilhelm Ludolf Gerhard Augustin, Baron von. (1730-1794). Personal *Papers Collection (1780-1781)*. Library of Virginia Archives and Manuscripts Collection. Steuben was sent to Virginia to recruit and train a Continental regiment of 18-months men for use by Nathanael Greene's Southern Army. Steuben's appearance in Virginia was followed shortly afterward by Benedict Arnold's and William' Phillips' expeditions up the James River which interfered with Steuben's mission. He was named commanding officer of the Continental Army in Virginia and orchestrated military operations with the Virginia Militia until Lafayette arrived and took command. The collection on this reel contain letters regarding supplies, discipline and other aspects of the campaign.

Tucker, Frances. *Letter, Frances Tucker to St. George Tucker, 14 July 1781.* PDF of original in author's possession.

War Office. Great Britain. *Selected "Very Old Series" and "Old Series" Papers, 1776-1881.* Certificates of Birth, etc. – Loyal American and Canadian Corps. Public Record Office papers containing petitions from widows and former members of Tarleton's British Legion. Part of the Virginia Colonial Records Project accessed through the Library of Virginia.

War Office. Virginia. Journal. 18 January 1781 to 31 December 1781. War Volume 53. Miscellaneous Microfilm Reel 663. Library of Virginia Archives and Manuscripts Collection. The General Assembly passed an act in its May 1780 session creating the War Office to replace the Board of War, which was abolished. These records provide a daily journal of activities including letters sent, warrants, and orders issued, all connected with the business of providing goods and services in support of the military.

Wayne, Anthony. (1745-1796) *Personal Papers Collection.* 1781. Miscellaneous Microfilm Reel 769. Library of Virginia Archives and Manuscripts Collection. Wayne was in command of a regiment that consisted primarily of Pennsylvania Line with about four companies from Virginia when he entered Virginia in May 1781. This particular correspondence concerns the period from

April through October 1781. The letters outline the military actions which led to the siege of Yorktown.

Published Primary Sources
Agnew, Jean. *Some Wards of Nottoway Parish, Amelia County and Their Connections*, Genealogies of Virginia Families from the William and Mary College Quarterly Historical Magazine. (Baltimore, MD: Clearfield Publishing Co., Inc. 2006)

Campbell, Charles. Editor. The Bland Papers: Being a Selection from the Manuscripts of Colonel Theodorick Bland, Jr. (Petersburg, Va: Edmund & Julian C. Ruffin) 1840. Originally published in two volumes.

Dorman, Frederick. Editor. Virginia Revolutionary Pension Applications. Volumes 1-50 with indexes. Washington, D.C.: Dorman. 1958 to present. Alphabetical compilation of Virginia's Revolutionary War pension applications on file with the Federal government. The pension testimony often gives details on various combat actions, periods of militia service, routes of march and order of battle information.

Francisco, Peter. *Letter of Peter Francisco to the [Virginia] General Assembly*. 11 November 1820. William and Mary College Quarterly Historical Magazine. Vol. XIII (Richmond, Va: Whittet & Shepperson, General Printers) 1905; p217-219

-----. *Pension Application of Peter Francisco (W11021)*. Transcribed and annotated by C. Leon Harris (26 Feb 2014). Published Pension on website of Southern

Campaigns of the American Revolution, Southern Campaign Revolutionary War Pension Statements & Rosters (http://revwarapps.org/)

Gwathmey, John H., edited and compiled. <u>Historical Register of Virginians in the Revolution</u>. Richmond, VA: The Dietz Press. 1938. Complete list of identifiable Virginians with an existing record of service on the American side during the American Revolution.

Hanger, George, 4th Baron Coleraine, Major of the Cavalry of the British Legion and Captain in the Hessian Jaeger Corps. <u>In Reply to Strictures by Roderick McKenzie, late Lieutenant in the 71st Regiment on Tarleton's History of the Campaigns of 1780-1781</u>. London: Hanger. 1789. Library of Congress Call No. E236.T193.

Jefferson, Thomas. <u>Writings.</u> Edited by Merrill D. Peterson. New York: Literary Classics of the United States of America, Inc. 1984. Includes Jefferson's autobiography, *Notes on the State of Virginia*, Public Papers, Addresses, Messages and Replies, Miscellany and Letters.

Lafayette, Marquis de. <u>The Papers of the Marquis De Lafayette. Lafayette in the Age of the American Revolution. Selected Letters and Papers, 1776-1790</u>. Volume IV. April 1, 1781-December 23, 1781. Edited by Stanley J. Idzerda. Ithaca, NY: Cornell University Press, 1981. Excellent compilation of letters to and from Lafayette covering his participation in the 1781 Virginia campaign.

MacDonald, Kim; Michael Barton. *Cavalry of His Majesty's British Legion: Tarleton's Dragoons*. Huntingdon (1783). *Master Index*. Roster of Tarleton's Legion after exchanged or returned as prisoners of war. The men were granted lands to settle in Nova Scotia, specifically in Port Mouton, Guysborough County and St. Andrews, New Brunswick. This roster provided the names of men in the various companies of the British Legion. The website no longer exists however some rosters are available at *Oatmeal for the Foxhounds* website which is dedicated to all things Tarleton (http://home.golden.net/~marg/bansite/_entry.html) and *The Online Institute for Advanced Loyalist Studies* (http://www.royalprovincial.com/military/musters/britlegn/mrblmain.htm).

Palmer, William M., editor, Calendar of Virginia State Papers. Volumes II (1781) and III (1782). Richmond, VA: Commonwealth of Virginia. 1881. Reprint of official state papers for the periods indicated. Among the papers are correspondence between local and state government officials as well as letters from citizens to state officials.

Petersburg National Military Park. *British Military Operations in Virginia 1781*. Petersburg, VA: January 1934. Miscellaneous primary source manuscripts filed with the Dinwiddie Historical Committee.

Reese, George H., compiler. The Cornwallis Papers: Abstracts of Americana. Charlottesville, VA: University of Virginia Press. 1970. Published for the Virginia Independence Bicentennial Commission. This is a printed guide to the War Office and Pubic Record Office papers of Charles Cornwallis and the Virginia Campaign.

Saffell, W.T.R., editor. <u>Records of the Revolutionary War</u>. Baltimore: Genealogical Publishing Company. 169. Originally published in 1894. Transcripts of the Revolutionary War pension applications of Virginia militia men and some Continental soldiers.

Sanchez-Saavedra, E.M., compiler. <u>A Guide to Virginia Military Organizations in the American Revolution, 1774-1787.</u> Richmond, VA: VA State Library. 1978. This work gives background on Continental Regiments from Virginia with some limited information on militia participation in major battles.

<u>Southern Campaigns of the American Revolution</u> (www.southerncampaign.org). This is an excellent website that hosts transcribed pension applications of men who served in the Southern Campaigns. Pensions are searchable. It is hosted by the Kershaw County (SC) Historical Society.

Tarleton, Banastre. <u>A History of the Southern Campaigns of 1780-1781 in the Southern Provinces of North America</u>. London: 1787. A first edition of this work is in the special collections reading room of the Hampden-Sydney College Library. The work was reprinted in 1968 and also during the Bicentennial years.

Washington, George. <u>Diaries of George Washington,</u>

1771-1785. New York: Houghton-Mifflin Company. 1925. Regents Edition.

-------. The Writings of George Washington. Vol. 22. Washington, DC: Government Printing Office. 1937.

-------. *Washington Papers*. National Archives Founders Online. (http://founders.archives.gov/) Letter from Thomas Nelson, Jr. to George Washington, 27 July 1781.

Secondary Sources
Ailsworth, T.S.; Ann P. Keller; Luna B. Nichols and Barbara R. Walker. Comp. Charlotte County-Rich Indeed: A History from Prehistoric Times Through the Civil War. Charlotte County, VA: The Charlotte County Board of Supervisors. 1977.

Amelia County Historical Commission. Historical Notes on Amelia County. Kathleen Hadfield, editor. W Cary McConnaughy, associate editor. Salem, WV: Walsworth Don Mills Publishing. 1982.

American Revolution Bicentennial Office. Manuscript Sources in the Library of Congress for Research on the American Revolution. Washington: Library of Congress, 1975.

Anonymous. *Tarleton's Legion*. Collections. (Vol 29, p1-50). Nova Scotia Historical Society (undated). An abbreviated unit history to accompany a post-war roster of the British Legion given royal land grants in Nova Scotia. Accessed in 1999. Website no longer available.

Bell, Landon C. Cumberland Parish-Lunenburg County, VA 1746-1816, Vestry Book, 1746-1816. Richmond, VA: The William Byrd Press, Inc. 1930.

----. The Old Free State. Richmond, VA: The William Byrd Press, Inc. 1927.

Berkley, Edmund Jr. comp. Revolutionary America: Guide to Rare Books and Manuscripts Department in the University of Virginia Library. Charlottesville, VA: University of Virginia. 1977.

Boatner, Mark. Encyclopedia of the American Revolution. New York: David McKay Company, Inc. 1966.

Bodie, John Bennett. Seventeenth Century Isle of Wight. Chicago: Chicago Law Printing Company. 1938.

Bradshaw, H.C. History of Prince Edward County, Virginia. Richmond, VA: The Dietz Press, Inc. 1955.

Bracey, Susan L. Life by the Roaring Roanoke: A History of Mecklenburg County. Mecklenburg County, VA: The Mecklenburg County Bicentennial Commission. 1977.

Brown, Douglas Summers. Editor. Historical and Biographical Sketches of Greensville County, Va., 1650-1967. Emporia, VA: Riparian Woman's Club. 1968.

Brunswick County Bicentennial Commission. <u>Brunswick County, VA 1720-1975: The History of a Southside Virginia County</u>. Brunswick County, VA: Brunswick County Bicentennial Commission. 1976.

Capon, Lester J. Editor-in-Chief. <u>Atlas of Early American History, The Revolutionary Era 1760-1790</u>. New Jersey: Princeton University Press. 1976.

Duncan, Richard R. comp. <u>Theses and Dissertations on Virginia History: A Bibliography</u>. Richmond, VA: Virginia State Library. 1986.

Early, Ruth Hairston., <u>Campbell Chronicles and Family Sketches: Embracing the History of Campbell County, Virginia 1782-1926</u> (Lynchburg, Va: 1927)

Eckenrode, H.J. <u>The Revolution in Virginia</u>. Hampden, CT: Archon Book. 1964. Reprint of 1916 work. Chapter Ten (p261-275) deals with military operations in Virginia.

Fitzgerald, Sallie Hardaway. <u>Jottings About Nottoway</u>. Virginia Fitzgerald Jones, editor. Nottoway County, VA: Nottoway County Historical Association. 1972.

Gephardt, Ronald M. comp. <u>Revolutionary America 1763-1789</u>. Volumes I and II. Washington, DC: Library of Congress. 1984.

Haynes, Donald. Editor. <u>Virginiana in the Printed Book Collections of the Virginia State Library</u>. Volume II. Richmond, VA: VA State Library. 1975.

Higham, Robin. Editor. A Guide to the Sources of British Military History. Los Angeles: University of California Press. 1971.

Jefferson, Mary Armstrong. Old Homes and Buildings of Amelia County, Va. Volume I. Farmville, VA: Farmville (Herald) Printing. 1964.

Jones, Richard. Dinwiddie County: Carrefour of the Commonwealth, A History. Richmond, VA: Whittet and Shepperson. 1976.

Lutz, Francis Earle. The Prince George-Hopewell Story. Richmond, VA: The William Byrd Press, Inc. 1957.

Lumpkin, Henry. From Savannah to Yorktown: The American Revolutions in the South. New York: Paragon House Publishers. 1981.

Meade, William (Bishop) (1789-1862), Old Churches, Ministers and Families of Virginia, Vol. 1, (Philadelphia: J.B. Lippincott) 1857.

McConnaughy, Gibson Jefferson. Comp. Old Homes and Buildings of Amelia County, Va. Volume II. Amelia, VA: Mid-South Publishing Company. 1986.

Moon, W.A. Peter Francisco: The Portuguese Patriot. Pfafftown, NC: Colonial Publishers and Bradford Printing Service, Inc. 1980.

Natcher, Philip R. Encyclopedia of British, Provincial and Germany Army Units, 1775-1783. Harrisburg,

PA: Stackpole Books. 1973. A handbook on British military units serving in the American Revolution. Provides historical sketches of most units.

Richmond Dispatch.
---. *A Virginia Giant: Peter Francisco's Wonderful Record in Days of the Revolution.* 4 August 1901. Page 1.

---. *Peter Francisco.* 9 July 1897. Page 4.

Selby, John E. The Revolution in Virginia 1775-1783. Williamsburg, VA: The Colonial Williamsburg Foundation. 1988.

Stemper, Sol. The Bicentennial Guide to the American Revolution-The War in the South. Volume III. New York: E.P. Dutton & Company, Inc. 1974.

Swem, E.G. Virginia Historical Index in Two Volumes. Roanoke, VA: The Stone Printing and Manufacturing Company. 1936.

Watson, Walter A. Notes on Southside Virginia. *Bulletin of the Virginia State Library.* Vol. XV, (Richmond, Va: Superintendent of Public Printing) September 1925.

ABOUT THE AUTHOR

Greg Eanes holds a B.S. in Occupational Education from Southern Illinois University-Carbondale and a Master's in Military History from American Military University. A graduate of the Air War College and Air Command and Staff College he retired as a Colonel from the U.S. Air Force in 2011 after more than 34 years military service. He was in Operations DESERT SHIELD/DESERT STORM and post-9/11 combat operations in Iraq and Afghanistan

A former journalist and educator he has served on a variety of faculties and adjunct faculties to include the Air Force Intelligence School at Goodfellow AFB, Texas, the Defense Intelligence Agency's Joint Military Intelligence Training Center (Washington, DC), Randolph Henry High School (Charlotte County Public Schools) dual-enrollment program and as an adjunct for Patrick Henry Community College in Martinsville, Va.

Greg Eanes

Notes

[1] Cornwallis to Tarleton, 11 June 1781, *Cornwallis Papers*, PRO CO5/103, *Original Correspondence and Military Despatches, July-Nov 1781*; H.J. Eckenrode, The Revolution in Virginia (Hampden, CT: Archon Books, 1964) Chapter X, 261-275.

[2] Cornwallis to Clinton, 12 July 1781, *Cornwallis Papers*, Survey Report 04899, Reel 513, PRO 30/11/74, pages41-42, *Original Correspondence and Military Despatches, July-Nov 1781*. Cornwallis wrote, "The 23rd Light Company has done duty for some time past with the Legion, which is not returned from an incursion to the upper part of the country…I have therefore, in place of the 23rd, sent [to Portsmouth] the light infantry of the 80th. The enemy's army having come as low down the country and we having by the destruction of their [water] craft rendered it difficult for them to pass [the] James River below Tuckahoe…I thought it a good opportunity to endeavor to destroy the magazines between the James River and the Dan that are destined for the use of their Southern Army. I according detached Lt. Col. Tarleton with the Legion Cavalry and something upward of 100 mounted infantry on the 9th inst from Cobham [located at the modern Jamestown Ferry southern bank] with orders to call among other places at Prince Edward and Bedford Court House where I was informed their principal military stores had been collected. This will be a fatiguing expedition but I shall be able to give them rest upon their return as I've little appearance of cavalry being needed in this quarter for some time to come. In the meantime I shall remain at or near this place till he comes back which I hope will be in a few days. I have detached Lt. Col. Dundas with a part of the 80th to destroy shipping and stores at South Quay and if possible I shall send a detachment to Edenton for the same purpose, before I fall back to Portsmouth."; John Selby, The Revolution in Virginia 1775-1783 (Williamsburg, Va: Colonial Williamsburg Foundation, 1988) 179.

[3] Banastre Tarleton, Campaigns of 1780-81 In the Southern Provinces of North America (London: 1787) 402-403; see Note E, letter from Cornwallis to Tarleton dated, Cobham, July 8, 1781; a "puncheon" is a cask of 72 to 120 gallons.

[4] Mark Boatner, Encyclopedia of the American Revolution (New York: David McKay Company, 1966) 1174.

[5] W.D. James as quoted by Boatner, 1174.

[6] Pension of Benjamin Shenault (W6867).
[7] Pearse, W.H., Colonel <u>The Cavalry Journal</u>, Vol. 5, No. 17, (January 1910) 'General Sir Banastre Tarleton, BT., G.C.B. This quote was captured from the website *Oatmeal for the Foxhounds*, a site dedicated to Banastre Tarleton and the British Legion. It is managed by Marg Baskin who has done a tremendous job pulling together a wide range of primary source information on Tarleton; a 'one stop shop' for Tarleton history.
(http://home.golden.net/~marg/bansite/_entry.html)
[8] Philip R. Natcher, <u>Encyclopedia of British, Provincial and German Army Units 1775-1783</u>. (Harrisburg, Pa: Stackpole Books, 1973); Petition of John McKinney, British War Office, PRO 42/63, Reel 803, a trumpeter in Capt. Hovenden's Troop of the British Legion. McKinney's father served with the British against the French and was at Louisburg. The father settled near Albany, NY. McKinney said, "And when the American Rebellion broke out he was offered a [Rebel] Captain's Commission in order to drill their men, with which he would not comply, for which cause himself and family were drove away, his House and Barn burnt, and all his property destroyed; after suffering many hardships both father and son joined His Majesty's forces in Philadelphia…." They ended up in the Legion. The father was made Quartermaster Sergeant and the son trumpeter. McKinney says he joined in 1779 serving five years to the day. He was at Cowpens and Guilford C.H. He said that after Cowpens, Capt. Sir David Henlock sold his commission to Capt. Vernon who was a Lieutenant. The pension said, "This deponent further saith that the shattered remains of the British Legion came along with Lord Cornwallis from North Carolina to Virginia and that both Capt. Vernon and deponent were taken prisoners at Little York in Virginia."; see also Richard Jones, <u>Dinwiddie County: Carrefour of the Commonwealth, A History</u> (Richmond, Va: Whittet and Shepperson, 1976) 106.
[9] Henry Lumpkin. See order of battle strengths in appendix of <u>From Savannah to Yorktown: The American Revolution in the South</u>. (New York: Paragon Books, 1981) 296-299; Selby, <u>The Revolution in Virginia 1775-1783</u>, for Charlottesville numbers, 279; Cornwallis to Clinton, 17 July 1781, *Cornwallis Papers*, Survey Report 04899, Reel 513, PRO 30/11/74 pages 41-42, from Suffolk, Cornwallis says, "The 23rd light company has done duty

for some time past with the Legion, which is not yet returned from a mission to the upper part of the country."; See also PRO 5/103, Survey Report 491, Reel 67, p265/133. *'State of the Troops in Virginia Under the Command of Lt. General Earl Cornwallis'*, Return of Troops, dated 15 August 1781. The return, taken about two weeks after the conclusion of Tarleton's Southside raid, show the Legion with a total strength of 206 fit for duty. This included one Lt. Col., four Captains, six Lieutenants, three Ensigns, one each of Adjutant, Surgeon and Surgeon's mate, three quartermasters, 13 Sergeants, six drummers and 186 rank and file. About 105 men were listed absent within or without the district suggesting they were on detached duties, while seven were identified as sick and one wounded. Those classified as 'Prisoners with the Rebels' were 16 Sergeants, eight drummers and 253 rank and file. Total listed at 35 Sergeants, 17 drummers and 513 rank and file. The vast majority of the prisoners were captured at Cowpens. The 23rd Regiment of Foot reported two Captain, five Lieutenants, one each Ensign, Adjutant and Surgeon, 15 Sergeants, three drummers and 156 rank and file for a total of 184 fit for duty They reported 27 as prisoners of war, 71 sick, and 53 wounded for a total strength of 24 Sergeants, 16 drummers and 347 ranks and file. According to an analysis of British Legion muster rolls conducted by Donald J. Gara and posted on *The On-Line Institute for Advanced Loyalist Studies*, there was no Legion Infantry after Cowpens. They were either transferred to the Legion cavalry or sent to Charleston, SC where they stayed until the end of the war. See http://www.royalprovincial.com/military/rhist/britlegn/blcav1.htm (Miscellaneous Notes).

[10] Tarleton, Campaigns, 358-359.

[11] War Office. Virginia. *Journal.* July 11, 1781; *Journal of the War Office*, 18 January 1781 to December 1781, War Volume No. 53, Microfilm Reel 900, Virginia State Library and Archives Collection.

[12] *Legislative Petitions of the General Assembly, 1776-1865*, Accession No. 36121, Box 3, Folder 11, Petition of Daniel Jones, Library of Virginia Digital Collections; see also Watson, Notes, 60. Jones petitioned the House of Delegates for rebuilding the mill and granary in 1787. These had been located on the 'Chair Road', present day Rt. 619. Oral tradition from the area says the road

was named 'Chair Road' because it was just wide enough to accommodate a one-seat carriage of that period.

[13] Walter A. Watson, Notes on Southside Virginia. (Richmond, Va: Bulletin of the Virginia State Library, 1925), 60. Reprinted in 1979. No evidence has been found of any such destruction at the courthouse.

[14] Watson, Notes, p56

[15] Watson, Notes, 59.

[16] Jean Agnew, *Some Wards of Nottoway Parish, Amelia County and Their Connections*, Genealogies of Virginia Families from the William and Mary College Quarterly Historical Magazine. (Baltimore, MD: Clearfield Publishing Co., Inc. 2006) 408.

[17] Sallie Hardaway Fitzgerald. Jottings About Nottoway, edited by Virginia Fitzgerald Jordan. (Blackstone, Va: Nottoway County Historical Association, 1972) 13.

[18] Watson, Notes, 60. Colonel William Craddock was Judge Watson's maternal great-great-great-grandfather. He lived on the Dr. George Scott property outside of present day Crewe.

[19] Watson, Notes, 60; W.A. Moon, Peter Francisco: The Portuguese Patriot. (Pfafftown, NC: Colonial Publishers and Bradford Printing Service, Inc., 1980) 16, quoting Henry Howe, Historical Collections of Virginia (Charleston, SC: Babcock & Co., 1846)

[20] Moon, Peter Francisco, 17-18.

[21] Moon, Peter Francisco, 95-97; Learn more about Peter Francisco at the *Society of the Descendants of Peter Francisco* webpage (http://www.peterfrancisco.org/aboutus.php).

[22] Francisco's Fight with Tarleton's Dragoons reportedly occurred within a few feet of the front steps where the 1931 Daughters of the American Revolution was originally placed. The monument was moved closer to the main road to make it easy for tourists to locate. A fire destroyed the home on the night of Saturday, 12 April 1902. The photo in this work is from Genealogies of Virginia Families from the William and Mary College Quarterly Historical Magazine. Reprint by Clearfield Company, Inc., Genealogical Publishing Co., Inc, (Baltimore, Md, 2006) p410. According to the 1931 WPA Virginia Historic Site Survey, the home was also used as a Confederate hospital during the Civil War. According to The Record of Hampden-Sydney College, Vol. 5, Issue 4, (1931), p14, "When the marker was dedicated

Judge Lewis Epes of Blackstone accepted the marker on behalf of Nottoway County. Hampden-Sydney College Professor F.H. Hart, head of the Department of History made the principal address of the occasion."; see also Virginia Historical Survey Reports VHIR/20/0162 and 0163 written by H.E. Rorer, 22 June 1936. The DAR stone marker reads as follows: "Here at West Creek, Peter Francisco captured single handed Nine of Tarleton's Dragoons, July 1781".

[23] It was called Miller's Tavern at the time of the Revolution.
[24] *The Farmville Herald*, Vol. 17, No. 26, 12 April 1907, 'Patrick Henry and John Randolph in Prince Edward', p3
[25] Jean Agnew, *Some Wards of Nottoway Parish, Amelia County*, 408-409. This information is based on testimony of Miss Lizzie Ward who recorded the family's story. According to Agnew, "Miss Lizzie strongly expressed her indignation at Peter Francisco's 'greatly exaggerated' version of that West Creek encounter which is quoted by Howe in his History of Virginia. She said it was proven at the time that Benjamin Ward was a patriot." Ward died in 1783 at the age of 35 after reportedly falling from one of the British horses that he kept.
[26] *Richmond Enquirer*, 4 August 1901, 'A Virginia Giant', p1 & 16.
[27] *Isaac Chapman Pension* as recorded by Frederick Dorman, Va Revolutionary War Pension Applications. (Washington, DC: 1958) Volumes 1-50.
[28] Watson, Notes, 158.
[29] Kathleen Hadfield and Cary McConnaughy, Historical Notes on Amelia County (Salem, WV: Walsworth Don Mills Publishing, 1982) 39; *Cornwallis Papers*, passim; John H. Gwathmey, Historical Register of Virginians in the Revolution (Richmond: The Dietz Press, 1938)
[30] Watson, Notes, 60, quoting his grandmother.
[31] Washington. The Writings of George Washington. Vol. 22 (Washington, DC: The Government Printing Office, 1937) 368.
[32] Pension of Jesse Stegall (S7646).
[33] Pension of Joseph Baugh (R21837).
[34] H.C. Bradshaw, History of Prince Edward County, Va. (Richmond, Va.: The Dietz Press, Inc. 1955) 124-125.
[35] Receipt of John Calbreath, *Harry Innes Papers. Commissary Papers, May 1781-February 1782.* Library of Congress Collections. Item 174

[36] Record Book of John Morton. *John Morton Papers*. Library of Congress Collection. Morton was the Deputy Commissary in Prince Edward County, Va.; *Amelia County Order Book, 1780-1781*. There are no entries between the Amelia Court's 26 April 1781 meeting and the 27 September 1781 meeting. At the 26 April meeting at least one wagon and team were furnished to the County Commissioner for Continental or State use. By 1782 Amelia County began certifying claims for payment for the government's impressments of goods and services from county citizens. Many of the claims are for the use of wagons, horse teams, and the hire of teamsters. Unfortunately a vast majority of the claims fail to give dates of impressments therefore it cannot be determined when and in relation to which campaign the impressments were made.

[37] Bradshaw, Prince Edward, 739. Bradshaw says a 1780 letter of McRobert's has a dateline of Providence suggesting the place was probably named before the Tarleton incident.

[38] McRobert Letter. Calendar of Virginia State Papers. Edited and arranged by William M. Palmer (Richmond, Va: Commonwealth of Virginia, 1881) 2:308-309.

[39] Dr. J.D. Eggleston, *'Historic Slate Hill Plantation in Virginia'*, Bulletin of Hampden-Sydney College, October 1945, 14-16; Bradshaw, Prince Edward, 740. According to Bradshaw, "When threatened with being shot if she did not reveal her husband's whereabouts, Mrs. Venable said, 'Go ahead and shoot. My husband's life is more valuable to his country than mine'."

[40] Ibid, 435, quoting Howe; The Davidson incident may have taken place at the Briery River Bridge just south of Worsham, the old Prince Edward Court House site.

[41] John Hatchett, Prince Edward County, Va: A Short Narrative of the Life of John Hatchett, undated publication of Hampden-Sydney College President J.D. Eggleston "from an old manuscript loaned me by Mrs. Louise Leonard."

[42] Bradshaw, Prince Edward, 740.

[43] Bradshaw, Prince Edward, 741. Bradshaw says, "One finds the substance of this story related in several Southern communities about the Revolution.

[44] Eggleston, Slate Hill, 14-16.

[45] Pension statements of Thomas McDearman (S5749), of Amelia, "he…was engaged as a volunteer in reconnoitering

parties until the last of July [Banastre Tarleton] was at that time passing through the Country."; Abner Foster (W8823), "The company to which this declarant belonged was detailed off from the main body of the regiment (his former regiment in the first tour of service[Col Thomas Meriwether]) to act as a guard to the county of Amelia and to watch the movements of [Banastre Tarleton] who was there with his legion hovering on the borders of Amelia."; Josiah Jackson (W9332); John Thurmond (R10585) served under Capt. Charles Allen of Prince Edward County. "That the company was raised for the purpose of pursuing Colonel Tarlton [Banastre Tarleton] the British officer who has passed through the said County of Prince Edward & that he marched in the company under Captain Charles Allen in pursuit of Colonel Tarleton from Prince Edward County through Amelia County down to Petersburg where they were stationed a few days and there Captain received information that Tarleton had joined Cornwallis...."

[46] Journals of the Council of the State of Virginia. Volume II, October 6, 1777-November 30, 1781. (Richmond, Va: Division of Purchase and Printing, 1932) 35.

[47] Pension of James Roberson (Robinson) (S14333). He said they remained "several days until the baggage came up and then marched down to Petersburg, where they crossed the river & marched up to Manchester & crossed James River to Richmond...."

[48] Calendar, 2:220

[49] Lafayette to Wayne, 15 July 1781. *Wayne Papers*. Lafayette added, "You may write to Mr. Constable at Petersburg who will try to get you more intelligence of the enemy's situation below you—But I think they are gone to Portsmouth."; Lafayette to Wayne, 15 July 1781, Lafayette in the Age of the American Revolution: Selected Letters and papers, 1776-1790. Volume IV, April 1, 1781 – December 23, 1781. Edited by Stanley J. Idzerda. (Ithaca, NY: Cornell University Press, 1981) 248-249; Wayne was to march from his camp at Four Mile Creek; Lafayette to Morgan, 16 July 1781, Selected Letters, 251. Morgan's dragoons consisted of the Maryland Volunteer Cavalry and Major John Nelson's Detachment of Virginia State Cavalry. The Marylanders were from Baltimore and Frederick Counties under Nicholas Moore and John Ross Key, respectively. The Marylanders consisted of

about 70 dragoons.
[50] War Office. Virginia. *Journal.* 15 July 1781.
[51] Lafayette to Washington, 20 July 1781. Selected Letters. 255-256, "General Waine's Pennsylvanians Never Exceeded about 700. Fighting and Desertion Have Much Reduced them. I have Sent Him to Goode's Bridge upon Appomattox. The three Pennsylvania Batallions Have been Reduced to two – about 250 fit for duty. To this I have added 300 Virginia New levies. General Morgan and 500 Riflemen with Some dragoons is also at Goode's Bridge to Support Waine."; Ibid, 255, "So Soon as He [Cornwallis] Had Crossed [the James River] He Improved the Opportunity to Send Tarleton in Amelia – But was Disapointed in the Stores which He expected to find, and which Had Been Previously Removed. I thought at first the Cavalry would join Rawden [in South Carolina], and detached Waine and Morgan Either to Maneuvre Tarleton Down or to Determine His Course...He [Tarleton] Retired with Precipitation towards Portsmouth Where the British Army is for the Present."; Dr. Richard C. Bush, III, *"The End of Colonel Gaskin's War, May-October 1781"*, Bulletin of the Northumberland County Historical Society, Vol. XXXIII-1996; Dorman, Pension applications of Ebenezer Flanagan (v37, p69), Peter Bertrug (v6, p77), James Caruthers (v16, p64), Thomas Caul or Call (v17,p28) and William Givens (v44, p33). Among Morgan's militia was a brigade of three regiments under General William Campbell. The regiment consisted of a large contingent of Augusta County men (perhaps 200) under the commands of Col. Thomas Hugart and Lt.Col. John McCreery.
[52] Lafayette to Parker, 18 July 1781, Virginia Historical Magazine, Vol. 22, p262; Selected Letters, 256. Lafayette to Washington, 20 July 1781. Lafayette reported Parker had about 300 men in his command. Lafayette said, "I have directed Parker's Detachment, about 300 militia, to keep clear of Danger from an attak. (sic) His men are from adjacent Counties to Suffolk." He also reported "a post at Sandy Point to Examine the Ennemy's (sic) Movements" and some militia in the vicinity of Williamsburg, probably under Lt. Col. James Innes, as well as Gloucester militia "in their own county." All the latter were tasked to keep tabs on the main British army.
[53] Dorman, Pension of Harrison Ashworth, V3, p34-35.

[54] Ibid

[55] *Letter Frances Tucker to St. George Tucker, 14 July 1781.* PDF of original in author's possession.

[56] Ibid. Frances Bland Randolph Tucker was living at Bizarre, the former Randolph Plantation near present day Farmville; Philemon Holcombe was a Prince Edward County militia officer commanding a cavalry detachment.

[57] Letter, St. George Tucker to Theodorick Bland, 17 July 1781. The Bland Papers: Being a Selection from the Manuscripts of Colonel Theodorick Bland, Jr. (Petersburg, Va: Edmund & Julian C. Ruffin) 1840, p74.

[58] T.S. Ailsworth, Charlotte County-Rich Indeed: A History from Prehistoric Times Through the Civil War (Charlotte Court House: The Charlotte County Board of Supervisors, 1977) 329. The Colonial militia reportedly drilled at McKinney's field at McKinney's Old Store.

[59] Ailsworth, Charlotte County, 329.

[60] Calendar, 2:222; Journal of the Council of the State of Virginia, Vol. II, 357; Ibid, 358-359, Lafayette wanted to "Fix lines of riders at proper distances" to act as relay riders; Lafayette to Washington, 20 July 1781. Selected Letters, 256. "I have obtained from the Executive that 2,000 Militia Be ordered to Boyd's ferry upon Dan River. This force will Give General Greene a Decided Superiority." These militia were to be picked up and incorporated into Wayne's force on his way south.

[61] Calendar, 2:263. Col. Davies to Gov. Thomas Nelson, July 23, 1781; A Guide to the Old Dominion (Works Project Administration Project, New York: Oxford University Press, 1976 reprint) 515.

[62] Calendar, 2:231. Capt. Ambrose Bohannon to Col. Davies, July 20, 1781, Irvin's Store; see also 2:220; see also Ruth Hairston Early, Campbell Chronicles and Family Sketches: Embracing the History of Campbell County, Virginia 1782-1926 (Lynchburg, Va: 1927) 33.

[63] Pensions: John Pullin (S3750) "the enemy did not as was anticipated march to New London to destroy the magazine"; Samuel Mathews (S5732), "I was called out when Tarlton [Banastre Tarleton] was expected to attack the magazine at New London then in the county of Bedford in Virginia and served three weeks at New London aforesaid under Colonel Charles

Lynch; after Tarleton retired we were discharged having served three weeks as before mentioned."; Charles Russell (S46067), guarded the "Magazine" noting "there was about one hundred and fifty men employed, he thinks the command of that place was under a certain Col. Smith, he was employed most of said three months in Guarding said Magazine and part of the time in removing said magazine to the woods to keep the British from Blowing it up." Discharged August 1781; Oliver Porter (S32452), "he volunteered & served two days in guarding military stores from Prince Edward county to New London in Bedford...to prevent them from falling into the hands of the enemy."

[64] Calendar, 2:310-311, Capt. Nathan Reid to Col. Davies, August 10, 1781

[65] Campbell Chronicles and Family Sketches: Embracing the History of Campbell County, Virginia 1782-1926 (Lynchburg, Va: 1927) by Ruth Hairston Early, p.33

[66] Tarleton, Campaigns, 358-359; Calendar, 2:234, Wooding to Col. Davies, Halifax, July 21, 1781.

[67] Bradshaw, Prince Edward, 741. Citing Hatchett and Ailsworth, 322; Bush, *"The End of Colonel Gaskin's War"*; McAllister pension declarations, John Hogg (No. 38) states Muhlenberg's, Wagner's and Campbell's Brigades were at the bridge. Hogg was in the Light Infantry Company of Capt. Woodford, Lt. Ruffin and Ensign Bacon of Muhlenberg's command. Morgan was the overall commander for the Virginia Militia. The exact movement into Amelia has not been determined.

[68] Lafayette to Morgan, 17 July 1781. Selected Letters, 253.

[69] Wayne to General Thomas Nelson, 24 July 1781, Goode's Bridge. *Wayne Papers*.

[70] Susan L. Bracey, Life By the Roaring Roanoke-A History of Mecklenburg County (Mecklenburg County, Va: The Mecklenburg Bicentennial Commission, 1977) 82-83. She was citing State Records, Vol. XV, 553 and Hill, 126. Reported to be Lewis Burwell who lived in the northwest corner of the county, the area of Finneywood above present day Chase City.

[71] Bracey, Mecklenburg, 82-83. Citing State Records, Vol. XV, p586, Capt. Sam Chapman to General Sumner, 19 July 1781.

[72] Calendar, 2:240-241, July 23, 1781, Garland to Gov. Nelson.

[73] Calendar, 2:245, ltr dtd July 24, 1781 from Lunenburg County Lieutenant N. Hobson and Others to Col. William Davies in reply

to his circular letter of 15 July.

[74] Calendar, 2:323-324; Landon C. Bell, The Old Free State (Richmond, Va: The William Byrd Press, Inc., 1927) 255-256.

[75] Landon C. Bell (1880-1960), The Old Free State: A Contribution to the History of Lunenburg County and Southside Virginia, (Baltimore, Md: Genealogical Pub. Co.) 1974, 254-256. Bell cites Bishop William Meade (1789-1862), Old Churches, Ministers and Families of Virginia, Vol. 1, (Philadelphia: J.B. Lippincott) 1857, 484-485 and Henry Howe (1816-1893), Virginia, Its History and Antiquities, (Charleston, SC: Babcock & Co) 1845, 359.

[76] Meade, Old Churches, 484-485

[77] William Read Turner, Old Homes and Families in Nottoway (Blackstone, VA: Nottoway Publishing Company, 932) 9-10. Turner says Edmondson's became known as Burnt Ordinary and afterwards was sold by John McCrae to Capt. Samuel Morgan and became known as Morgansville; Jones, Dinwiddie, 209.

[78] Calendar, 2:261, Col. John Jones of Brunswick County to Gov. Thomas Nelson, July 27, 1781; Brunswick Times Gazette, October 6, 1955; Department of Historic Resources, undated clipping, 'Another Version of How Smokey Ordinary Was Named', "At a point on the Nottoway River about six miles below Route 1, they cut down the banks and crossed over. The bridge built later here has been called Cutbank."

[79] Francis Earle Lutz, The Prince George-Hopewell Story (Richmond, Va: The William Byrd Press, Inc. 1957) 94. The entire quotation reads as follows: "Before Cornwallis reluctantly gave up his futile chase of the elusive Lafayette and started his march eastward to effect a junction with a British Fleet with reinforcements and supplies, he sent another raiding force into Prince George in August. It was on this occasion that the courthouse and its contents were put to flames and the irreplaceable records were either destroyed or carried off." No primary source is cited for this information. I found no record of a British raid to Virginia's interior in August suggesting the writer was in error to the actual time of the operation.

[80] Calendar, 3:113, Augustus Claiborne of Sussex County to Col. Davies, 28 March 1781; WPA Project, Sussex County: A Tale of Three Centuries (Sussex County School Board, 1942) 54 citing Calendar 3:113.

[81] Ibid.
[82] *North Carolina History Project* citing Michael Hill, editor, The Governors of North Carolina (Raleigh, 2007); William S. Powell, North Carolina Through Four Centuries (Chapel Hill, 1989); and Milton Read, The Tar Heel State: A History of North Carolina (Columbia, 2006) (http://www.northcarolinahistory.org/encyclopedia/399/entry/).
[83] *Thomas Burke Papers, 1763-1852*, Collection 00104, Wilson Library, UNC-Chapel Hill (afterwards Burke Papers). Letter, Bannister to Burke, 8 July 1781.
[84] *Burke Papers*, Col. Josiah Parker to Burke, cc to General Green, from Crocker's Isle of Wight County, 14 July 1781.
[85] *Burke Papers*, Long to Jones, 16 July 1781.
[86] *Burke Papers*, Dixon to Long, 17 July 1781.
[87] *Burke Papers*, Burke to Lock, 18 July 1781.
[88] Pension of Charles Holt (W7756). Holt was from Granville County in company of Capt. John Peace. He says they were stationed at Taylor's Ferry for about one month.
[89] *Burke Papers*, Burke to General Butler, 18 July 1781.
[90] Pension of Henry Sparrow (S31384). Sparrow was placed on guard at Taylor's Ferry about this time. See also Pension of James F. Hudgins (S8740); See Pension of Isaac Roberts (S19453). The magazine was at Banks Old Store at Taylor's Ferry.
[91] *Burke Papers*, Burke to Commanding Officers in Franklin and Warren Counties. He said expect no more a month's service.
[92] *Burke Papers*, Burke to Southern Counties in Virginia, 18 July 1781; Nuttbush was a small settlement along Nuttbush Creek. It is on the site of present day Williamsboro in Vance County, NC.
[93] *Burke Papers*, Burke to Nathanael Greene, 18 July 1781.
[94] *Burke Papers*, Letterbook, Vol. I, July 10-20, 1781. Burke to Virginia Governor Thomas Nelson, 19 July 1781; In a 20 July letter to a Colonel Williams, Burke notes of the raiders: "They destroyed all the mills, and collected all the horses and saddles in their rout."
[95] War Office. *Journal*. July 19, 1781.
[96] George Washington. *Diaries*. July 29, 1781, 246
[97] *Cornwallis Papers*, abstracts, 182.
[98] John Bennett Bodie, 'Isle of Wight Miscellany', Seventeenth Century Isle of Wight (Chicago: Chicago Law Printing Company, 1938) 176.

[99] Sol Stemper, The Bicentennial Guide to the American Revolution-The War in the South, Vol. III (New York: E.P. Dutton and Company, Saturday Review Press, 1974) 179
[100] Jones, Dinwiddie, 94. See Calendar of Events.
[101] *Wayne Papers*. Wayne to Lafayette, 22 July 1781.
[102] *Wayne Papers*. Wayne to Nelson, Goode's Bridge, 24 July 1781. Intelligence information on British movements were a constant concern for the American forces. The British had control of the seas and could move at will. To counter these movements the American forces had to conduct forced marches. As a result many units were in constant movement responding to real and imagined British Army threats. Lafayette wrote to Wayne, "every intelligence but that of one deserter affirms, that Lord Cornwallis and Tarleton are with the fleet. When a general has nothing but horse and foot to calculate an enemy, that flies with the wind, and is not within the reach of spies or reconnoitering he must forcibly walk in the dark."; Ibid, Lafayette to Wayne, 4 August 1781. Wayne remained at the Goode's Bridge encampment through July 29 and attempted to obtain much needed supplies, specifically shoes and clothes. At one point Wayne confiscated 173 pair of shoes, 11 pair of boots and some clothing material from Virginia state supplies. Virginia authorities protested to Lafayette. Wayne wrote, "There is neither arms or a single article of clothing [in] all this country; our people are barefoote and bare legged rather high up. For God's sake forward shoes and overalls with all possible dispatch, if one pair of either would save this Army or America from destruction, they could not be found in the Antient Dominion."; Ibid, Wayne to Irvine, 29 July 1781; see also Lafayette, Selected Letters, correspondence of Nelson to Lafayette, 03 August 1781; *Wayne Papers*. Lafayette at Malvern Hill to Wayne, 29 July 1781.
While the Goode's Bridge camp is not described, Lafayette wrote to Wayne saying, "Your position at Goode's Bridge is, I am told, very pleasant...."
[103] Calendar, 2:235. Price to Pryor, New London, July 22, 1781.
[104] Ibid, 2:240, Pryor to Davies, Charlottesville, July 23, 1781.
[105] *Cornwallis Papers*, Nelson to Cornwallis, 23 July 1781.
[106] *Burke Papers*, Parker to General Jones
[107] Calendar, 2:258-259, Nelson to Washington, 27 July 1781.
[108] *Cornwallis Papers*, Cornwallis to Nelson, 6 August 1781,

[109] Ibid, Cornwallis to O'Hara, 14 August 1781.
[110] Ibid, Nelson to Cornwallis, 3 September 1781.
[111] Ibid, Cornwallis to Nelson, 8 September 1781. Many of Cornwallis' drafts were recopied by an aide for his signature. The drafts often include information that was deleted for the final copy therefore they provide a little more information. The September 8 letter is an example. The draft notes it was Tarleton who made the decision to keep Archer and Royall. The final copy states only the commanding officer at Portsmouth made the determination. This absolved Tarleton from receiving the blame and possible repercussions.
[112] Watson, Notes, 154; Virginia Magazine of History and Biography (V35) 444, Obit of Major Peter Field Archer which noted "his father was made a prisoner in Amelia County and conveyed to Portsmouth, where he was seized with small pox, of which disease he died."
[113] Natcher, Encyclopedia. Survivors of the Legion stationed in Charleston, South Carolina and in New York were merged into the King's American Dragoons and placed on the British establishment for regulars on December 25, 1782.
[114] Tarleton, Campaigns, 358-359.
[115] Lafayette to Wayne, 25 July 1781. Lafayette, Selected Letters, 277; also note 1 quoting Gottshalk, Letters of Lafayette, 211; Lafayette to Washington, 20 July 1781. Selected Letters, 259. Casualties are based on documented incidents involving Francisco's fight, the Prince Edward Briery Creek incident and the Taylor's Ferry incident.
[116] Lafayette to Greene, 23 July 1781. Lafayette Selected Letters, 269. "I Have lately Understood Tarleton's designe was to destroy iron works and Some other Matters up the Country which our detachment Has timely prevented." see also p274, to Wayne, 23 July 1781. "I have lately Understood that Tarleton's object was to destroy Mr. Ross's Works and Many Valuable Stores up the Country which Has Been prevented By Your Crossing the River."
[117] Calendar, 3:684, *Petition of the Inhabitants of the County of Amelia to his Excellency Thomas Nelson, Jr., Governor and the Honourable Council of the State of Virginia*, undated, 1781; Calendar, 2:240-241, David Garland of Lunenburg to Governor Nelson, 23 July 1781; Calendar, 2:261, Col. John Jones of Brunswick to Gov. Nelson 27 July 1781.

Made in the USA
Charleston, SC
09 January 2015